Democracy
in the
Fifty States

Kim Quaile Hill

Democracy
in the
Fifty States

University of Nebraska Press

Lincoln and London

© 1994 by the
University of Nebraska Press
All rights reserved
Manufactured in the United States of America
⊚ The paper in this book meets
the minimum requirements of American National
Standard for Information Sciences—
Permanence of Paper for Printed Library Materials,
ANSI Z39.48–1984.
Library of Congress Cataloging in Publication Data
Hill, Kim Quaile, 1946–
Democracy in the fifty states / Kim Quaile Hill.
p.   cm.
ISBN 0-8032-2372-2 (cloth : acid-free paper)
1. State governments–United States.
2. Democracy–United States–States. I. Title.
II. Title: Democracy in the 50 states.
JK2408.H54   1994
324′.0973–dc20
94-1604
CIP

Contents

Illustrations

Figures

Introduction

The British scholar James Bryce once wrote of the United States, "No nation ever embarked on its career with happier auguries for the success of popular government." Throughout our history Americans have been preoccupied with the extent to which we have achieved that goal. Many scholars and political observers have explored the matter. Their deliberations range across every stripe of ideology, explore every possible related topic, offer a host of rewarding insights, and, inevitably, reach divergent ends and conclusions. Controversy rather than consensus prevails here.

In my judgment there are two, differently flawed camps into which the bulk of the systematic writing on democracy in the United States falls. In the first group are books that have evidence but no conclusions. These books, in other words, explore in great detail the various components of government relevant to democracy, but they venture no judgment about the whole that is composed of those parts. The typical political science textbook is of this character—providing lengthy discussions of all the nuts and bolts of government but seldom offering a characterization of the entire machine.

Second, there are books that have conclusions but no evidence. There are innumerable popular and scholarly writings, that is, that begin with an assumption about the condition—usually the poor condition—of U.S. democracy and then proceed to offer either an explanation of the problem or a set of proposals for extricating our-selves from whatever political mess is alleged.

The present book attempts to bridge the gap between these two approaches to the study of government, and I believe that its conclu-sions and its suggested directions for future inquiry are far more sat-isfactory than those I have described here. In this book I pose a seemingly naive question: if we take a straightforward definition of democratic government and compare U.S. state governments with it, how well do they fare? That test illustrates some provocative differ-ences in the extent to which the fifty states are democratic. Thus I reject both the typical scholar's reticence to offer far-reaching conclu-sions without yet more evidence and the typical ideologue's readiness to do so on the basis of only scant evidence. My guiding assumptions are that democracy can be defined relatively precisely and that actual governments can be fairly compared on the basis of the definition. I recognize, too, and take account of the dramatic changes in U.S. state governments since World War II that affect these comparisons. We have made remarkable progress with respect to some require-ments for democracy, such as the right to vote, but we have indeed suffered notable reverses in other areas while experiencing little pro-gress in still others. The remarkable political events of the second half of the twentieth century, then, make this study especially timely.

Among the additional motivations for this book, the first arises from my assessment of the extant *empirical* scholarship relevant to the democratic process in the United States. The bulk of contempo-rary, empirical political science research on American politics is con-cerned with one or another aspect of the democratic process. Yet because the political process encompasses a number of linkages among citizens, elites, and government institutions, any given schol-ar can choose to focus on a variety of particular topics that ultimately relate to this broad concern. Such scholarship is also characterized by a common orientation: the "normal science" desire to examine only

one part of the overall political system or political process at a time—
and to do so in microscopic detail. This orientation is wise and fruit-
ful as a base upon which broader research can eventually build.

To date, however, no scholarship has taken the latter step with respect to the study of democracy in the United States. That is, no
scholar has attempted a comprehensive assessment, based on sound
and complete empirical analysis, of the extent to which the fifty state
governments are indeed democratic and of the consequences of whatever degree of democratization they have achieved. This book offers
a comprehensive, empirical, theory-based analysis of the extent to
which the governments of the fifty states can be judged to be democratic and of the public policy consequences of the degree to which
they are democratic. Thus the book is intended to build upon prior,
normal science scholarship and to contribute to our *general* knowledge of U.S. political processes.

The focus on state governments in this study deserves at least brief
explanation here, too, even though it is also discussed in detail in
chapter 1. In brief, the number and diversity of the state governments
offer an opportunity for comparative assessment of U.S. political
processes that is not feasible for other levels of government. There is
a good deal of evidence, as well, that the states differ considerably in
the extent to which their governments approximate the democratic
ideal. If we find that some states indeed approach that ideal, we
would have the basis for investigation of the roots of that success—
which might be useful for generalizing to the nation at large.

This book also extends a large body of comparative state politics
research that has microscopically probed the nuts and bolts of the
democratic process in the states in the best tradition of normal science. That literature provides a profitable base for the present work,
but it offers contradictory clues about the health of democracy in the
individual states. Some of that scholarship indicates that a vigorous
democratic process exists in these governments. Other scholarship

suggests that the state policy process exhibits far more qualified democratic linkages. Building on this work, my findings advance it toward a more comprehensive understanding of state politics.

There are other motivations, as well, for this study. There exists in some quarters today a disillusionment with representative democracy in America, the form of democracy by which our state governments supposedly operate. Some "normal science" students have been led to question the vigor or success of this form of government. And there is a large and influential body of political theory that concludes that representative democracy has failed to realize its intended ends. Scholarship in the latter vein recommends some form of participatory democracy to replace or supplement our existing institutions of government, thereby to achieve a more thoroughgoing democratic process. Beyond criticism in the scholarly community, many average Americans are also cynical about the success of representative democracy.

Yet I believe these critics have been too hasty in judging contemporary political processes. Without the benefit of a comprehensive, empirical assessment of the democratic process, they may misperceive some ways in which representative institutions work rather well. Some of these critics, that is, may be writing books with conclusions but no evidence, to repeat my earlier phrase. Further, the most insightful of these critics recognize that even participatory democracy must exist in concert with healthy representative mechanisms. Thus the specifics of how the latter mechanisms work well or ill, and of how their workings might be improved, are matters of importance even for those who would advance the cause of participatory democracy.

This book first proposes and carries out an empirical assessment of the extent of representative democracy in the states. That assessment is guided by empirical democratic theory and its explication of the essential components of such a governmental system: equal rights to vote in free and fair elections, competitiveness among political parties contending to control government through those elections, and the degree of mass participation in elections. Second, this analysis is replicated for two time periods chosen for their historical distinctiveness in terms of the development of modern democracy in the states: the late 1940s and the early 1980s. (A detailed explication of why these periods were chosen follows in chapter 1.) Third, the book offers extended descriptive assessments of each of the components of democracy and of how states achieved each of these components in the two periods under study.

I also include a good deal of historical background on the evolution of voting rights, party competition, and mass participation before the 1940s, as critical and comparative perspectives by which to judge my evaluations of the states for the first period under study here. Similarly, consideration of relevant political events and changes between the 1940s and the 1980s provides a more informed perspective by which to judge my assessments of democratization for the latter period.

All these "component" assessments of voting rights, competition, and participation—and the empirical analyses that undergird them— are then combined to produce comprehensive measures of democracy in the states for each of the two time periods. And for those readers skeptical of how satisfactory this approach is in measuring such a complex concept as democratization, I offer a systematic, empirical demonstration of the validity and reliability of the comprehensive measures.

These analyses yield interval-level measures of democratization that can be employed in subsequent theory tests. They also allow me to develop ordinal groupings of states into commonsensical categories (polyarchic, oligarchic, and other types of government that are precisely defined here), which will have more intuitive meaning for many readers. The latter groupings are discussed, as are their implications for the everyday political life of states that fall into the different categories.

There is one further bit of skepticism about representative democracy that this book addresses: does democracy "deliver the goods"?

More precisely, many critics allege that representative democracy does not lead to the degree of public control of government or the kind of public policies that they believe it should. (The range of such criticism is difficult to summarize because critics differ in terms of their expectations for representative democracy.) Careful statements of empirical democratic theory, however, provide specific hypotheses about how the more-democratic governments differ from the less-democratic ones in terms of their public policy orientations. Drawing upon such theory, I find strong empirical support for two of its most central propositions: the more-democratic states adopt more equitable policies in providing for the welfare of the less fortunate and they ensure a greater range of civil rights. And these conclusions, I should add, take account of federal government influence on state policies in these two areas and of the most prominent other influences on state policies indicated in prior research.

The principal motivations for this book were scholarly, as described above. Yet the purpose of such work is not simply to sustain a dialogue with other scholars. I also wish to advance general public understanding of the governmental process. Thus it is my hope that this work will be of interest to a variety of audiences, including scholars, students, and lay readers. Normal science examinations of small segments of the democratic process, though very important, seldom arouse the interest of the latter two audiences. A comprehensive study of the democratic process might well do so. For that reason I have attempted in this book to escape the tedium of the typical scholarly work. I rely on the work of a host of other scholars for the foundations of my own work here, and I employ the intellectual methods of scientific inquiry. But I have used academic jargon sparingly and have kept my citations to scholarly literature to the most essential and illustrative works, while employing empirical analyses in a careful—and carefully explained—manner. And I have attempted to write in a way that enlivens, instead of deadens, the subject at hand, which is admittedly a large task for any writer worth his or her scholarly salt.

In this enterprise I have also benefited from a variety of personal, professional, and material assistance. My spouse, Patricia Hurley, offered unstinting encouragement to stick with the project. Her own academic research interest in related matters led to considerable professional assistance with the intellectual development of the book, too. Larry Dodd offered general encouragement and advice about the project, as well, over much of its life. Chandler Davidson and Joseph Stewart read and commented quite constructively on chapter 2. Bryan Jones and Norman Luttbeg read and critiqued the entire manuscript before I sent it out for review. Jonathan Nagler offered useful statistical advice for some of the analyses. Earlier versions of chapters 5 and 6 were presented, respectively, at annual meetings of the Southern Political Science Association and the American Political Science Association. Commentators on those panels, especially Thomas Dye, offered useful critiques of, and encouragement for, the work. Finally, Robert Albritton and Robert L. Savage, who reviewed the manuscript for the University of Nebraska Press, offered a number of useful ideas for improving some of the arguments and their presentation in this book.

The work for the book was supported by grants from the Advanced Research Program of the Texas Higher Education Coordinating Board and from the University of Houston–Clear Lake. Texas A&M University provided considerable material support, too. Some of the data employed in chapter 4 were made available, through Texas A&M University, by the Interuniversity Consortium for Political and Social Research.

Democracy
in the
Fifty States

1

Is There Democracy in America?

Did you, too, O friend, suppose democracy was only for elections, for poli-
tics, and for a party name? I say democracy is only of use there that it may
pass on and come to its flower and fruits in manners, in the highest forms of
interaction between men, and their belief—in religion, literature, colleges,
and schools—democracy in all public and private life.

Walt Whitman

The United States of America has a democratic government. All
Americans know this, too, for we have heard it all our lives. Our
parents called it that. Our courses in civic education called it that—
instructing us, at the same time, in the responsibilities of the democratic citizen. Government officials, too, use this term as the standard label for our political system. Even political science scholars
routinely characterize our nation as democratic. At one time or another we have been presented in scholarly literature as the first modern nation that became truly democratic, as the leader (in one or
another sense) of the other democratic nations in the modern world,
and as the model for many nations governed under other schemes that
have democratic ambitions. The recent breakdown of a host of communist regimes and the struggle of many of those nations to achieve
democratization have made our government an even more prominent

example of democracy. U.S. advice on governing has been actively sought by the leaders of many of these nations.

Yet are we truly democratic? I suspect that every citizen is at times skeptical about this matter. All of us have observed government policies we judged not to be supported by the majority of Americans. We have at times doubted the power of "the people" as opposed to that of one or another special interest. We have been suspicious of the motives of various public officials, questioning, in effect, their commitment to the public interest.

Doubtless, many Americans are cynical about the truth of our democratic rhetoric. Such doubts have led many of them to ignore their responsibilities as citizens. If the system is not truly democratic, they might reason, of what possible importance is their participation in it?

Despite the casual way scholars sometimes describe America as a democratic nation, there is controversy in their ranks as well about the accuracy of that description. The mildest scholarly criticism observes what are thought to be modest or temporary lapses from democratic standards: public participation in politics that is judged too low, but not critically so; occasional unresponsiveness of government to the public will; or individual instances of the power of special interests that eclipse general preferences. Behind such criticism is the assumption that, at least over the long run, government generally follows public preferences. The system may not be perfectly democratic, but it is sufficiently so to merit that label with only modest qualification.

There are, however, considerably stronger intellectual attacks on our government. At the most extreme, Marxist critics see a government controlled by the economic elite, the capitalist class. The forms and appearances of democratic procedure are but rituals, these scholars argue, meant to delude the average American into believing the myth of democracy. The ruling class and its minions in government manipulate those rituals and control the government's agenda and policies from behind the scenes. The goals of government are to ensure the maintenance of the capitalist system and the position of the ruling class within it.

Most Americans would be uncomfortable with this Marxist critique, although many would be so mainly because of the label it carries. Marxism is associated with evil, rival powers like the former Soviet Union, not with an intellectual approach for explaining how societies are governed. Many Americans would be uncomfortable, too, with the prescription offered by some of the Marxist critics: capitalist control of American government can be overthrown only via a socialist revolution.

At the same time many average Americans and many non-Marxist scholars are critical of U.S. inequalities of political power that appear to favor the wealthy, in particular corporate America. The subversive power of special interests is often lambasted at the average American's dinner table as well as at communist cabals. And a notable number of non-Marxist scholars have offered less extreme arguments about how economic power leads to disproportionate political power. There are, then, a variety of popular and scholarly critiques of our government that center on inequalities of wealth as substantial threats to democracy.

Glib and widespread rhetoric to the contrary, then, many Americans are uncertain about just how democratic their government is. Too often, however, we approach this matter casually and superficially. We must go beyond rhetoric to reality. And we must be systematic in our thinking about what democracy is supposed to be—as well as about how closely our governments approximate that standard. To assess how democratic are the governments of the fifty states, we must first define democracy.

What a Democracy Is

A form of government as widely celebrated and embraced as democracy would seem easy to define. Every scholar and schoolchild understands its essence to be government by the people, yet there is considerable diversity in how democracy is specifically defined, even in scholarly writings. We should first be specific ourselves about what a democracy is. I believe that we should acknowledge one of the preferred definitions straightaway: that of Ranney and Kendall (1956: 18–39). According to this formulation, democracy has four essential elements:

Popular sovereignty. Governmental power is vested in the people at large.

Popular equality. The power to influence government is shared equally by all citizens.

Popular consultation. Government officeholders must periodically ascertain the public preference for government policy and must then follow that preference.

Majority rule. When members of the public cannot agree on policy, the majority preference prevails.

Two facts should be emphasized about this definition. First, it characterizes an *ideal;* a government cannot be democratic unless it enjoys all four of these traits without qualification. Even if only one of the four is compromised, the government is not democratic but something else. Whether any government can actually attain this ideal is a matter we will consider later in this chapter. Second, this definition—and all other proper ones, in my view—includes requirements only for the *procedures* by which government operates (see Huntington, 1991: 5–13). It says nothing about the wisdom of government decisions and nothing about the goals that government should pursue. Democratic rule is determined by the majority of equally empowered citizens. Even if the majority makes foolish choices, the society may still be governed democratically. The only exception is that the majority cannot alter procedures that guarantee the four requirements listed above. If the majority restricts the political rights of a minority, for example, it compromises the requirement for popular equality and, hence, the democracy itself.

4

The Procedures versus the Results of Democracy

The definition of democracy I have cited will not satisfy everyone, nor will it by itself serve all the needs of this book. There are various reasons why it is difficult to reach consensus on any single definition of democracy. One of these problems is that some people want to include in the definition a requirement for the goal of democratic governmental policy. The quotation from Walt Whitman at the beginning of this chapter reflects this view. Consider as another example the definition proposed by William H. Riker (1965: 31): "Democracy is a system of government in which the rulers are fully responsible to the ruled in order to realize self-respect for everybody." Consider, finally, John Dewey's (1937: 457) definition:

> Democracy is much broader than a special political form, a method of conducting government, of making laws and carrying on governmental administration by means of popular suffrage and elected officers. It is that, of course. But it is something broader and deeper than that. The political and governmental phase of democracy is a means, the best means so far found, for realizing ends that lie in the wide domain of human relationships and the development of human personality.... The keynote of democracy as a way of life may be expressed as the necessity for the participation of every mature human being in formation of the values that regulate the living of men together."

We might hope that such lofty goals would be embraced by democracies, but realization of the goals is not essential for democratic government to exist. The essence of democracy, once again, is popular control of government through particular procedures. At the same time, the goals expressed by Whitman, Riker, Dewey, and the like should not be casually cast aside. They represent the *promise* of democracy: what we hope will be the consequences of having a truly democratic government. If we can ensure that there is popular control of government, then this promise may be fulfilled. We cannot be

5

certain of fulfillment but popular control is the only possible avenue to it. As Dewey suggests, the democratic promise can only be realized if democratic procedures come first.

Direct versus Representative Democracy

A second problem in defining democracy is one of situation: the circumstances in which such governments might flourish and the possible effect of different circumstances on the form of democracy. Our dilemma here arises because some would compare larger polities to the models of the Greek city-states and of New England town meetings. These forms of government have been labeled *direct* democracy because all the eligible citizenry participated in major policy decisions. Of course, Greek democracy was seriously restricted because the participating citizens were limited to the male members of a small ruling class that presided over a larger number of slaves and resident aliens. The men of that ruling class met regularly to make governmental decisions collectively and, at least within their own number, democratically. Early New England town government operated under similar class and gender restrictions on the suffrage (Sly, 1930: 46–51).

The difficulty with these models is, of course, deciding how they might apply to far more populous and diverse modern societies. Not all Americans can meet together and collectively make government decisions. Nor, for that matter, can all Texans, New Yorkers, or Idahoans. There are too many of us, and there are too many decisions that must be made by government. Partly in recognition of this fact, all modern nations that presume to be democracies have adopted instead *representative* democratic mechanisms (see Dahl, 1989: 24–36, 213–24, for a brief discussion of the evolution of representative democracy). We elect officials to legislative and executive positions to make policy decisions in response to mass preferences. A small number of citizens acts in our name and, presumably, for our interests.

Disillusionment with Representative Democracy

Representative democracy necessitates a compromise with respect to the degree and character of "popular sovereignty." The inevitability of that compromise has been understood, as well, from the first use of this form of government, even though it has always provoked a good deal of criticism. Some critics, however, argue that representative democratic institutions have sunk to a remarkable level of unpopularity in the United States in recent years. There are clear signs that point to such disillusionment, as expressed by the comments at the beginning of this chapter, about how thoughtful Americans question the extent to which our governments are democratic. Public opinion polls over the last twenty years or so have offered objective evidence of low public confidence in governmental institutions and officials. And many people interpret sagging voter turnout in U.S. elections over the same period to indicate this critical mood, as well. Futurist John Naisbitt captured the sense of this criticism in his book *Megatrends* (1982). Naisbitt argued that direct democracy would become the dominant form of government in America because "we have outlived the historical usefulness of representative democracy and we all sense intuitively that it is obsolete" (160).

Naisbitt and other popular critics of representative democracy are supported by a good number of scholarly fellow-travelers. In fact, there is something of a "growth industry" of scholars proposing various versions of direct democracy for America. Benjamin R. Barber (1984) proposes a system he calls *strong democracy*. John Burnheim (1985) offers an alternative he calls *demarchy*. Samuel Bowles and Herbert Gintis (1986) and Carol C. Gould (1988) offer still other variations. These theorists believe either that representative democracy has failed to be truly democratic or that it simply cannot be so, and they believe that the practical barriers to direct democracy can be overcome.

Direct democracy is surely more thoroughly democratic than the representative version. But these critics may be too hasty in con-

7

cluding that representative democracy is a failure. The motivating assumption of this book is that representative democracy has actually prospered at certain times and in certain places in the United States. If we understand the character of those times and places, we may be able to use that knowledge in invigorating representative democracy elsewhere today. In effect, these critics may have based their arguments for a new order on conclusions about the failure of the present system for which there is insufficient evidence.

Furthermore, healthy representative democracy may even be a prerequisite to, or a necessary component of, direct democracy. The more thoughtful of the critics adopt this view, as well. Benjamin Barber (1984: 262) says his proposed institutions of *strong democracy* "should complement and be compatible with the primary representative institutions of large-scale modern societies." Carol C. Gould (1988: 258) goes even further, acknowledging that the institutions of representative democracy are essential parts of the larger system of direct democracy she proposes. And if representative democratic mechanisms are essential to the success of a direct democracy, then this book is as important to the proponents of the latter form of government as it is to those who believe that only representative democratic mechanisms are possible. We must know when and how representative institutions can prosper even if our primary goal is to ensure a fully developed system of direct governance.

There are other good reasons, too, to concern ourselves with the workings of representative democracy instead of writing it off summarily as a failure. The American public, however disillusioned it might be, favors representative democracy. Evidence of that fact comes from an unlikely source: Thomas E. Cronin's book *Direct Democracy* (1989), a seminal analysis of the workings of direct democracy mechanisms like the initiative, referendum, and recall in state governments. Cronin argues, based on public opinion data, that Americans want the majority of government policy decisions to be made through representative mechanisms even though they would like to have greater opportunities to use the initiative, referendum, and recall. As Cronin (1989: 228) concludes: "Legislatures are more important today than ever, as growing population and growing demands on government force them to assume greater responsibilities. Americans overwhelmingly endorse leaving the job of making laws to their elected representatives and view direct democracy devices almost entirely as a last alternative to the legislative process."

Doubtless, tensions and practical difficulties complicate representative democracy. How can elected officials be sure of public preferences? How can we ensure that officials will follow those preferences? What discretion, if any, should they be allowed in making decisions? There are no easy answers to any of these questions, and concern about each of them has generated a wealth of scholarly analysis. Yet representative governmental mechanisms are a practical necessity in all large modern societies, despite concerns about which procedures will ensure democracy and, for that matter, about how democratic such a government can actually be. Such concerns are prominent throughout this book.

The Specific Requirements for Representative Democracy

Government by the people is a glorious but inexact specification. Popular sovereignty, popular equality, and the other requirements laid down by Ranney and Kendall are equally abstract. How do we recognize popular sovereignty when it confronts us? How, that is, do we proceed from an abstract to a specific definition?[1] In the Greek city-states and in the New England town meeting, all "citizens" could participate directly in government decisions—thus popular sovereignty could be directly observed in practice. Indeed, in both systems the popular component in each of Ranney and Kendall's four criteria could be seen in operation.

To assess the quality of the representative democratic process, we must first specify a list of criteria for the procedures by which such a government operates, criteria that are concrete and readily observable. These requirements should also embody the principal meaning of the four abstract standards laid down by Ranney and Kendall. We may not be able to specify criteria that incorporate every nuance and implication of those four standards, but we can identify a set of necessary if not entirely sufficient requirements.

To anticipate the essential requirements of representative democracy, consider once again the character of large modern societies. Such societies—whether entire nations or states within the U.S. federal system—impose significant constraints on democratic government. Their size alone means that direct democracy is not possible. Hence, indirect means of public control of government take on special importance. Elections, in particular, are crucial, for they are the only practical means for the vast majority of citizens to participate collectively in government. Thus opportunities for electoral participation, the extent to which the public uses those opportunities, and the nature of election contests are critical to democracy.

Large societies also pose another problem: how to aggregate the political views of individual citizens so that they can be effectively transmitted to public officials and candidates for election. Given the practical constraint that not all members of the society can meet together and discuss policy choices, there must be institutions that promote this aggregation. Because political parties have characteristically served in this role, the character of these organizations and the manner in which they function are also critical to the working of democracy.

Taking account of observations like these, numerous scholars have offered lists of the requirements for representative democracy. Those lists differ, at least in their minor details, from scholar to scholar. Yet in the empirical research on democracy there is a consensus about the most essential, specific traits of a representative democracy. On every scholar's list (for example, Dahl, 1971; Downs, 1957: 23-24; Ranney and Kendall, 1956: 18-39), the core elements are:

Equal political rights to influence the political process on the part of essentially all adult citizens, including the right to vote, to express political views openly, to run for public office, and to form political groups that oppose the ruling regime. Most important of these is the right to vote—to participate in the election of those who will actually run the government.

Other individual rights are also ensured by constitutional or statutory law today, including a number of specific religious, social, and legal guarantees. Still others, especially those based on a desire for equality of economic opportunity, are frequently advocated. Many of these are widely held to be essential modern freedoms; some are more controversial. The most critical rights for the preservation of democratic government, however, are the ones that concern participation in the policy decisions of government through the election process.

Free and fair elections, regularly held, where the citizens elect by majority vote those representatives who will make specific policy choices in their name.

Participation in elections by the vast majority of citizens. The necessity of high public participation for democracy is, admittedly, somewhat controversial. Some have attributed low public participation—especially low turnout in elections—to either public satisfaction with or apathy toward government (see, as an example, Berelson et al., 1954). Hence, low participation could even be interpreted as a sign of high democratization. Others have argued that public participation levels are unrelated to democratization because high turnout may occur under thoroughly undemocratic regimes and conditions (Bollen, 1991).

Yet there are sound arguments that high participation is essential for democracy. It is explicitly or implicitly recognized as such in the definitions of a host of scholars. Further, Jackman (1987) has provided remarkable evidence that rates of participation in elections are shaped by a nation's political institutions and voting laws. Thus participation levels are not the product of political culture, of satisfaction with, apathy toward, or alienation from the political system. The influence, instead, of political institutions and laws means that turnout rates are determined by procedural aspects of the political regime. For that reason, and in keeping with the arguments I have advanced about the importance of procedures for the definition of democracy, Jackman concludes that turnout rates are important indicators of the level of "participatory political democracy."

Competing nongovernmental institutions that organize groups of like-minded citizens and articulate their policy preferences to government. Political parties have been especially venerated for carrying out this task. Indeed, some consider them absolutely essential to modern, representative democracy. Parties play a critical role within the government as well as outside it. Not only do they mobilize like-minded voters; they also organize the government itself by constituting groups of like-minded elected officials to shape policies and programs.

A critical element of this fourth criterion, however, is effective competition among the organized groups. There must be two or more political parties that can contest elections and form governments on a relatively equal footing.

These four traits capture the essence of virtually all definitions of representative democracy. No doubt, some readers might wish to add one or another additional stipulation or requirement, but a government that satisfied all four of the preceding traits perfectly would indeed be highly democratic; here we have practical, observable criteria by which to judge real governments. As I will demonstrate in chapter 5, we can also use these criteria to develop a highly valid and reliable measure of the degree of overall democratization of individual governments.

What Might We Have If Not Democracy

The requirements listed above for a democratic system are highly demanding of citizens, government leaders, and institutions alike. They may be so demanding that they are impossible to attain. The scholar Robert A. Dahl (1971, 1989) has argued that we should best think of such requirements, even of democratic government itself, as ideals for which real governments might strive but are unlikely to achieve completely.

Dahl goes on, however, to argue that some governments at least approach these ideals. While they fall short in one or another respect, a handful of governments around the world rate relatively highly in all these traits, at least most of the time. Dahl believes we should call them polyarchies, meaning governments "that have been substantially popularized and liberalized, that is, highly inclusive and extensively open to public contestation [for control of government]" (Dahl, 1971: 8). Polyarchies are not true democracies, and giving them a distinctive definition and label helps resolve difficulties in defining and judging our governments fairly.[2] Dahl's primary intention in using this alternative definition is to describe the governments of nations, and he counts the United States as a long-standing polyarchy; thus, by inference, he would judge the governments of the fifty states similarly.

The polyarchy is a somewhat more forgiving conception of how government in the United States might function. It recognizes the likely gap between the rhetoric of democracy and the reality of contemporary government, but it is still highly demanding. Governments must come close to the democratic ideal to qualify as polyarchies. Even if we do not have democracy, we may have *polyarchy*.

There is, however, a strong and diverse body of criticism that contends that even the polyarchic view of U.S. government is too charitable. In the view of these critics we do not simply fall short of true democracy—we fail entirely. With respect to the most important issues of government policy, these critics would say that it is not the general public but a select elite of our society that is in control. There are several versions of this thesis, hence several conceptions of the ruling elite.

Marxist scholars, as observed previously, argue that dominance by a tiny economic elite is inevitable in a capitalistic society like that of the United States. The ruling elite or class, in this view, is that small group that largely monopolizes the ownership of capital. Thus, in accordance with Karl Marx's general view of power, this capitalist, or corporate capitalist, class holds the assets necessary for the dominant means of economic production. Marxists differ among themselves over the details of how the power of this elite is ensured, but they agree on its existence.[3]

Others argue that some kind of elite control, if not strictly capitalist control, of U.S. government is inevitable. Joseph Schumpeter (1942: 250–83), for example, argues that government officials themselves constitute an elite that makes major policy decisions with considerable discretion. In this view the people at large choose government officials but exercise little control over them. C. Wright Mills, in *The Power Elite* (1956), envisioned an elite triumvirate—from business, government, and the military—that controlled major public policy decisions. In *Beyond the Ruling Class* Suzanne Keller (1963) argued that a number of "strategic elites" whose power was based on their social or professional positions, and sometimes on their expertise, shared the power to control society and government. Thomas R. Dye offers a contemporary explication of a similarly diverse, but quite exclusive and convergent, elite in *Who's Running America?* (1986).

Finally, there is a long tradition of scholarship that associates economic power with political power in the United States. Beginning with Charles Beard's classic, *An Economic Interpretation of the Constitution of the United States* (1914), a host of observers has noted the traditional deference of U.S. governments to private economic power, the disparities in such power in our society, and the ability of groups with such power to exercise disproportionate control over government. The latter view recognizes a kind of economic dominance of government, but by a larger and far more heterogeneous "elite" than that envisioned by the Marxists and most of the other elite theorists alluded to above.

A good deal of scholarship, sometimes entirely outside any of the preceding strains of elite theory, offers reasons why the latter view might be accurate. Research on participation in U.S. politics, for example, has found that a large portion of the public falls short of its civic duty as required for democratic government. Many Americans pay scant attention at best to political affairs, have little factual understanding of current policy issues, and seldom participate in the governmental process. Limited public involvement leaves considerable opportunity for those who are interested and active to determine the political agenda. Research on political participation also shows that the greater one's wealth, the higher the probability of active involvement in political affairs (see, among many others, Verba and Nie, 1987). Wealthy individuals and corporations take advantage of the opportunity to shape the political agenda.

Other scholarship has pointed out examples of how the behavior of public officials and of institutions like political parties sometimes falls short of democratic requirements, too. Taken together, all this evidence leads many observers to conclude that political power is unequally distributed to a high degree in our nation, and that the distribution of power favors the economically advantaged. What might exist, then, would be not democracy but an *economic oligarchy*. The appearance of democracy would be a facade, behind which is rule by an elite whose political power is based on economic position and resources.

Why the State-centered Focus?

Some might be puzzled by my focus on the politics of individual states instead of the nation at large. There are, in my judgment, important

15

benefits of the former approach that have been neglected by previous work on democracy in the United States. The rationale for my focus recognizes that the states are, in fact, separate governmental and political entities—by the dictates of their constitutions and by the place ensured for them in the U.S. Constitution.

The federal government in the twentieth century may have taken over many of the former powers of the states, but they still retain many important policy functions. State constitutions establish separate governments and what are, on the surface at least, democratic procedures for the operation of those governments and for decisions about state policy functions. If democracy exists in America, it surely exists at the state level. Yet there are good reasons to question the extent to which some states are democratic.

One of those reasons is the character of the social and community values that predominate in each state. (The extent to which the states are communities in the most literal sense is debatable, of course, but no more so than for the nation itself.) Thinking of the states in terms of community values recognizes that each one is distinguished by the political values of the groups that settled there, by what has come to be known as the "political culture." State political cultures are relatively distinctive, and they are an important influence on political affairs (Elazar, 1984). In particular, some of these cultural orientations prize and promote democratic processes; others do not. Georgia *is* fundamentally different from Minnesota in these terms, just as many Americans suspect. On the basis of cultural values alone, we might thus expect considerable differences among the states in the degree to which their political routines are democratic.

Over time, as a result of the interplay of indigenous political values and distinctive historical events, the states have developed extragovernmental political routines and institutions that also shape the character of their politics. Of special importance here are state political party systems. We do not have a two-party system in the United states. We have fifty party systems: fifty Republican parties and fifty

Democratic parties, with each pair of parties and the resulting party "system" unique to each particular state. Further, there are states where internal politics are still dominated by a single political party, while others exhibit vigorous two-party competition. Thus the historical evolution of the party system in each state has also affected the extent to which it is democratic.

Other historical developments have shaped the general extent of mass participation in politics and the exercise of political rights by minorities in particular. To reiterate, then, a state's progress toward democracy is the product of these several historical forces and experiences. The considerable differences among the states in terms of these experiences must explain, at least in part, why their progress toward democracy is highly variable.

Even on the basis of anecdotal evidence it is clear that there are, indeed, remarkable differences among the states on all the components of democracy. Voter turnout in elections provides some remarkable illustrations of this point. In presidential elections during the 1980s, for example, two-thirds of the voting-age population of Minnesota consistently voted. Yet in Georgia, Hawaii, Nevada, and South Carolina only about 40 percent of the voting-age public did so. Voting in statewide elections for governors and state legislatures mirrors this range of variation. Further, fewer than half the states can today be judged to have effective two-party competition in state-level politics, and the number enjoying that competition has not increased notably in the last twenty years. Such variations have always characterized state politics, but scholarly research has neglected their implications for democratization nationwide.

Sorting out differences in the level of democracy among the states should lead us, then, to some especially useful assessments of government in the United States. A straightforward accounting of our progress toward democracy should also encourage others to consider the actual variety among U.S. governments before offering sweeping generalizations about their character.

If we find that democracy is relatively healthy in some states and not in others, we will debunk the common assumption that whatever progress has been made in this direction has been shared nationally. Such a finding would also raise questions about the reasons for such differences and about the conditions in the states where democratic government flourishes. The fact that there are fifty states gives us a powerful intellectual advantage in carrying out comparative assessments. Using all fifty states as our "sample," we can explore the importance of a wide variety of social and political forces for democracy.

The Period under Study

Since the end of World War II a number of dramatic, divergent changes have occurred in American politics that are relevant to democracy; one could even argue that a revolution has occurred in the democratic process. I will examine the extent of democracy in the fifty states during both the late 1940s, the period preceding the revolution in the democratic process, and the 1980s, the period that followed it. I will thus be able to characterize both "prerevolutionary" and contemporary American democracy. I selected these two time periods on the basis of the relevant events that preceded and followed each one.

Between roughly 1960 and 1980, a literal revolution in political rights occurred (see chap. 2), giving millions of previously disenfranchised citizens the right to vote and otherwise participate in the governmental process. That change was largely the product of federal government intervention in voting rights policy, with the express purpose of making our political processes more democratic. Doubtless, too, that intervention has made this a more democratic nation.

Over much of the same period, however, some contrary changes also took place. Concomitant with the extension of voting rights to all citizens, there occurred a steady *decline* in overall public participation in politics. Voter participation in presidential elections, for example, rose to its post–World War II peak of 63 percent of the voting-age populace in 1960, but then it fell steadily, to about 53 percent in 1976, and has since remained in the range of 50 to 55 percent. A similar decline in turnout in state-level elections occurred over this same period. The decline in participation has made this a less democratic nation because of the high level of participation that is essential for democratic government.

Of equal concern for many observers has been the apparent weakening of the organizational capacities of political parties. The rise of candidate-centered elections—along with associated changes in voter, candidate, and party activities—has led some to fear the "decay" of U.S. political parties. They fear, that is, that parties might no longer serve their traditional functions of mobilizing large numbers of like-minded citizens, transmitting their preferences to government, and coordinating the actions of public officials elected under the party banner. In addition, there has been little progress toward increased two-party competition at the state level or in the U.S. Congress. The implications of these party, campaign, and competition trends for democracy are not entirely clear. The historical functions of parties have have been crucial for democracy, but those functions might be served in the future by other organizational mechanisms or by parties with other forms. For the short run, however, it is widely feared that both parties and the purposes they have traditionally served are at risk.

America has made dramatic strides toward democracy since World War II, but our progress has also been uneven. In some respects we may have become far less democratic. This book will attempt the first full assessment of the overall results of these tremendous changes by characterizing the degree of democracy in the states both before and afterward. In this fashion I will be able to indicate the nature and the degree of our progress toward democracy, as well as the specific locales where that progress is most advanced.

Chapters 2, 3, and 4 characterize the four separate component traits of democracy: political rights and free elections (chap. 2), political party competition (chap. 3), and public participation (chap. 4). These chapters rate each of the states for its progress toward democratization in both the late 1940s and the 1980s. There is a good deal of descriptive detail, too, about the historical and contemporary workings of each component of the democratic process. Chapter 5 summarizes the assessments of democratization in each state and each period, based on an aggregation of the various component ratings, and presents evidence on the scientific validity and reliability of these summary assessments. Chapter 6 addresses the effect of democracy on the governmental processes and policies of individual states, while chapter 7 offers conclusions about the findings of the book.

2

The Right to Vote

Who are to be the electors of the federal representatives? Not the rich, more than the poor; not the learned, more than the ignorant; not the haughty heirs of distinguished names, more than the humble sons of obscurity and unpropitious fortune. The electors are to be the great body of the people of the United States.

James Madison

The right to vote in free and fair elections is the most critical of democratic rights. Yet many Americans take this privilege for granted, even denigrating its importance. Some are more concerned with other rights—economic equality or the needs of particular groups such as women, the handicapped, the aged, and even the unborn. Nonetheless, it is the right to vote that makes possible the debate about other rights and liberties. Those with the right to vote have the most fundamental means to influence government policy. Those without it are excluded from much of the policy debate and, in times past, such people found their other civil liberties also at risk.

The right to vote is of interest for more than its instrumental value. It was secured for many Americans only in the last generation, suggesting how recent is some of our progress toward democracy. Our national mythology, of course, suggests we have been a democratic nation from the first. Have we not always chosen our public officials by elections? But the right to vote was highly restricted in the early days of the Republic. It was not until our nation's bicentennial celebration in 1976 that we could claim that this right was virtually universally shared, yet there still exist today impediments to its complete realization.

What have been, in fact, the status and evolution of the right to vote in the second half of the twentieth century? To what degree were voting rights assured in each of the fifty states in the two time periods under study in this book? These are the concerns of this chapter. As a preamble, we should recall the history of the extension of the suffrage up to the end of World War II.

The Evolution of Voting Rights in Law

At the time of the American Revolution and for a good number of years after the creation of the United States of America, the right to vote was a rare privilege. Each colony and, subsequently, each state prescribed its own laws on this subject, but their general character was quite similar, posing three major tests. First, only males were eligible. Second, only those who were free qualified. The latter test alone, by the way, excluded almost a third of the total population, those who were slaves and indentured servants (U.S. Commission on Civil Rights, 1959: 19). The final criterion was ownership of a stipulated amount of property or payment of a certain amount of taxes annually. On top of these universal criteria, some pre-Revolutionary colonies added tests of residence, citizenship, religious affiliation, or morality. As a result only a small fraction of Americans was even eligible to vote in the Colonial period or during the early Republic. The exact number of eligible voters is unknown, in good part because of the limitations of administrative records from this period. Yet popular vote totals from the 1824 presidential election—the first ones reported in contemporary U.S. government statistical documents— illustrate the restrictiveness of the franchise. Only about 19 percent of adult white males, or 8 percent of the adult population, cast ballots in that controversial contest between John Quincy Adams and Andrew Jackson.[1]

During the first half of the nineteenth century some of the barriers to voting fell. Jeffersonian and Jacksonian conceptions of popular democracy are generally credited with stirring a movement toward universal white male suffrage. Most property-owning and taxpaying requirements were relaxed, although they remained in effect in a handful of states. A few other limits, often intended to keep the suffrage from recent immigrants, remained valid or were adopted anew in some states. But generally speaking, free white male suffrage was fully achieved only by the time of the Civil War.

The broad grant of voting rights to the newly emancipated African American male citizens of the South after the Civil War proved to be short-lived. The defeat of the Confederacy and the passage of the Thirteenth, Fourteenth, and Fifteenth Amendments to the U.S. Constitution were the sources of this extension of voting rights. Briefly, the Thirteenth Amendment outlawed slavery, the Fourteenth guaranteed equal protection of the laws to all residents of the states, and the Fifteenth guaranteed the voting rights of citizens. These new laws were the first alteration of a major provision of the U.S. Constitution relevant to democratic rights. One of the celebrated compromises among those who drew up the Constitution was to let the states determine their own suffrage requirements. By means of this and other compromises, the Founding Fathers solved some of their greatest disagreements and secured ratification of the new basic law. Under the trio of Civil War–era amendments, the U.S. federal government, in effect, co-opted from the states some of the power to determine the suffrage.

Shortly after Reconstruction, however, the white majorities of the eleven former Confederate states regained control of their state governments and began to disfranchise African Americans by means of violence and intimidation and by such legal devices as literacy tests, poll taxes, grandfather clauses, and the white primary (Woodward,

23

1955; Key, 1949: 531–643; Kousser, 1974). In a sense this process proceeded slowly, depending on the intensity of political controversies that heightened white concern over the political power of African Americans. Yet by the turn of the century the vast majority of Southern African Americans had been effectively denied the right to vote by the state governments.

A good many Southern whites were disenfranchised in this process, as well, for poll taxes, literacy tests, and related suffrage restrictions affected many poor and lower-class citizens similarly, regardless of ethnicity. Key (1949: 542–50) and others offer persuasive evidence that such was the intention of some Southern political leaders, who wanted to minimize threats to their power from poor whites as well as from African Americans. Yet it was the African Americans who suffered most, for they were also subjected to widespread segregation in public and private facilities and to second- or third-class public services.

Between roughly 1850 and 1920 a number of non-Southern states also instituted literacy tests for voting. Some of the tests were intended to curtail the voting of new immigrants or of various ethnic minorities, while others were expressions of the idea that political rights ought to be based in part on some minimal educational attainment. These laws varied widely in their specific educational or literacy requirements and, hence, in their ultimate restrictiveness. Yet they represent a more limited perspective on individual rights than that which prevails today.

This restrictive view of voting rights had its share of "highly pedigreed" supporters. A leading textbook on U.S. government from this period, for example, observed of literacy tests for voting:

Assuming honest administration, there is much to be said for the literacy test. The electorate having now been expanded almost as far as possible, the next step would seem to be to "trim it at the edges" by eliminating the least intelligent. Ascertainment that a citizen can read and write no more guarantees that he will always vote wisely than testing an applicant for an automobile driver's license insures that he will invariably manage his car with safety for himself and others. But it is as effective a means as we have of debarring people who, by and large, are most likely to be unfit. And while at first glance the plan might seem undemocratic, and consequently out of harmony with American principles, the fact that all of the states now make it possible for practically any man or woman, even of low intelligence, to receive an elementary education without cost . . . relieves it of any opprobrium (Ogg and Ray, 1942: 170).

This argument would be compelling to many Americans today, but it ignores the reality of educational attainment in the 1940s and even later. In virtually all the states at that time, ethnic minorities such as African Americans, Native Americans, and Mexican Americans were systematically denied access to the educational opportunities available to the majority. And given the poverty and generally low social status of these groups, many of their number left school before achieving basic literacy. Thus even those who agree with Ogg and Ray must admit that when literacy requirements were imposed in states with large minority populations in the 1940s, the result was inevitably discrimination. Much the same reasoning was employed by the federal government when it suspended the use of all literacy tests for suffrage in the 1960s.

A number of states also traditionally denied the right to vote to Native Americans. Various arguments were advanced to support such laws. Some were based on constitutional ambiguities about the legal status of Native Americans. Others argued that Native Americans, being subject to tribal or federal law, were not a concern of state government, or that because those living on reservations were not subject to state taxation, they should not be allowed to participate in the affairs of the state governments (McCool, 1985: 105–16). In 1924, however, the federal government passed the Indian Citizenship Act, granting U.S. citizenship to all who were native-born. This act

25

brought Native Americans under the constitutional guarantees of the Fourteenth and Fifteenth Amendments, and all the arguments that had been used to disfranchise them were eventually set aside by the courts as unconstitutional. Nonetheless, Arizona and New Mexico continued to deny voting rights to Native Americans until 1948 (U.S. Commission on Civil Rights, 1961: 115-60).

Before World War II there was, of course, one other major extension of voting rights: to women. Nationwide, this grant was achieved by ratification of the Nineteenth Amendment to the Constitution in 1920. Previously, however, women had been granted the right to vote in thirty states (Scott and Scott, 1975: 166-68).

By the end of World War II there had also been some modest chipping away at the laws that disfranchised southern African Americans. The U.S. Supreme Court in 1944 outlawed all-white primary elections, which had denied any effective voting opportunity to those few African Americans who were allowed to register to vote in the South. Because the South was solidly one-party Democratic, the primary election for the Democrats was the only one where competition among candidates was a reality. In spite of the 1944 Supreme Court decision, however, the bulk of the southern suffrage restrictions put in place after Reconstruction remained in force even after World War II.

In summary, the United States had on the books by 1924 a set of suffrage laws that gave the appearance of true democracy for essentially all adult citizens. In accordance with the U.S. Constitution none of those laws could restrict the right to vote based on race, ethnicity, or gender (although those denying voting rights to Native Americans did precisely that). Yet restrictive laws and practices existed in a good number of states,[2] and the advocates of every restriction had a clever rationale to explain why literacy tests, poll taxes, white primaries, or other requirements were fair and wise. In many states, of course, the objective of these laws was quite different—precisely, to deny the logic of democracy. It must be emphasized that restrictions of the franchise were written into law by some state governments, which thus explicitly denied the right to vote to large numbers of Americans. They had created by law a nondemocratic form of government.

Many of the seemingly color-blind and class-blind suffrage laws were also enforced in a highly discriminatory manner. The records of the U.S. Civil Rights Commission, for example, document the selective and arbitrary enforcement by public officials of both suffrage laws and restrictions that went beyond those laws, with the intent of disfranchising ethnic minorities. Such discrimination, widespread in the South, existed in other parts of the nation as well. Heavy social pressures and threats of violence were also common in the South, adding still more barriers to the ballot box.

Not all states, of course, imposed such antidemocratic restrictions. Many had laudable records in pioneering the extension of the franchise and vigorously enforcing the laws that guaranteed the right to vote. There were thus considerable differences among the states in the late 1940s in the extent to which the right to vote was ensured.

Voting Rights in the 1940s

We can identify varying degrees of restrictiveness, and hence of antidemocratic bias, in the suffrage and election laws of the states in this period. Indeed, the bias ranges from what I will call moderately undemocratic to highly undemocratic systems of voting rights. The states can be ranked within this range by considering the particular types of franchise restriction operating in each one.

EXTENSIVE RESTRICTIONS ON VOTING RIGHTS
BASED ON ETHNICITY

The eleven Confederate states of the South enacted legal requirements for voter registration, such as poll taxes, literacy tests, and grandfather clauses, whose principal purpose was to restrict, if not deny entirely, the voting rights of ethnic minorities. Further, in all these states there was a regular pattern of selective enforcement of these laws to ensure that they achieved their purpose. On another level, widespread social oppression of minorities, operating through intimidation and physical violence, attempted to discourage African Americans and Mexican Americans, in particular, from exercising the right to vote.[3]

These laws and social practices have been widely documented. The curious reader might find of special interest the discussions of these problems written in the 1940s by Myrdal (1944), Bunche (1941), and Key (1949). Additionally, the annual reports, in particular, of the U.S. Commission on Civil Rights document the continued existence of these strictures on voting rights—and the underlying pattern of discrimination—well into the 1970s.

Restrictive franchise laws such as these would be critical for the democratic process regardless of the circumstances under which they arose, but they were particularly so in the South because of the size of the African American population. The effectiveness of these laws and practices can be seen in the minuscule numbers of African Americans who were able even to register to vote in the 1940s. Table 2.1 shows the percentages of the total population in the Confederate states that were African American in 1940, along with an estimate of what portion of voting-age African Americans were registered. One must conclude from these data that suffrage systems in this region were admirably constructed to deny the right to vote to sizable portions of American citizens.

Thus Alabama, Arkansas, Florida, Georgia, Louisiana, Mississippi, North Carolina, South Carolina, Tennessee, Texas, and Virginia must be labeled highly undemocratic in the 1940s in terms of the most elemental of requirements, the right to vote.

MODERATE RESTRICTIONS ON VOTING RIGHTS
BASED ON ETHNICITY OR LITERACY

During at least some portion of the 1940s seven states had laws that denied the right to vote to Native Americans. In five of the states the

Table 2.1. African American citizens and registered voters in the South in 1940

State	African Americans as a Percentage of State Population	Percentage of Voting-Age African Americans Registered to Vote
Alabama	35	Less than 0.5
Arkansas	25	3
Florida	27	3
Georgia	35	2
Louisiana	36	Less than 0.5
Mississippi	49	Less than 0.5
North Carolina	27	10
South Carolina	43	Less than 0.5
Tennessee	17	16
Texas	14	9
Virginia	25	5

Sources: U.S. Department of Commerce (1953: 36); Matthews and Prothro (1966: 148).

laws were apparently not enforced in this period (Bureau of Indian Affairs, 1948), but enforcement was the rule in Arizona and New Mexico. Native Americans gained the right to vote in the latter two states only after successful court challenges in 1948. Native Americans were sizable minority groups in both states, representing about 11 percent of the Arizona population and about 6 percent of that of New Mexico in 1940. For this reason these two states must be labeled as having moderately undemocratic suffrage systems.

A number of states in the 1940s imposed literacy tests for voter registration that might have had discriminatory effects. These states included Alabama, Arizona, California, Connecticut, Delaware,

Georgia, Louisiana, Maine, Massachusetts, Mississippi, New Hampshire, New York, North Carolina, Oregon, South Carolina, Virginia, Washington, and Wyoming (McGovney, 1949: 59–79). It is difficult to generalize, however, about the importance of these requirements as restrictive devices. They differed a good deal in terms of how the specific literacy or educational requirement was stipulated and in terms of the fairness of administration. In the South, as noted previously, they were used selectively to deny the right to vote to African Americans.

McGovney's (1949: 80–109) analysis of these laws and their apparent effect on voting turnout suggests that outside the South they were only modestly restrictive. In California, however, it was alleged that the English-language literacy test constituted a significant barrier for many in the state's large Mexican American community (U.S. Commission on Civil Rights, 1971). Indeed, the California Supreme Court ruled in *Castro v. California* in 1970 that this law violated the equal protection clause of the U.S. Constitution. Thus California may have had a moderately antidemocratic bias in its suffrage laws in the 1940s, but I have not found documentation to support this claim.

Based on the preceding assessment, then, only Arizona and New Mexico can be confidently placed in the category of moderately antidemocratic in the 1940s.

ANTIDEMOCRATIC MANIPULATION OF VOTES
BY POLITICAL MACHINES

A number of political machines of varying strength and importance still existed in the United States in the 1940s. These organizations controlled local politics in a city or a region by marshaling the support of large numbers of voters through the efforts of a network of party workers. The party workers were typically granted government jobs or similar perquisites as a reward for their efforts, and loyal voters, at least in some of the machines, could rely on party officials for access to local public services and for social and economic favors. In theory, then, voters, party workers, and party leaders all might derive material benefits from participation in the machine.

Machine politics is inherently undemocratic in the view of many observers. As Banfield and Wilson (1967: 125) argue about these organizations and their method of operation:

> A system of government based upon specific, material inducements is wholly at odds with that conception of democracy which says that decisions ought to be made on the basis of reasonable discussion about what the common good requires. Machine government is, essentially, a system of organized bribery.

One can see in political machines an element of undemocratic manipulation of the voters. At times, a voter's loyalty leads to no personal benefits, but there is at least potential benefit for both voter and elected official, and in some machines such advantages have been realized. It would thus be difficult to generalize about the influence of machine politics on the democratic process or to assess most individual machines in these terms.

In two states in the 1940s, however, there is substantial documentation that political machines operated to manipulate the votes of ethnic minorities in a clearly undemocratic fashion. In Texas and in New Mexico such organizations sustained the political power of the Anglo majority or of selected minority politicians while offering little in return to the manipulated voters (Fincher, 1974: 130–61; Holmes, 1967: 17–29; Key, 1949; Knowlton, 1962; Simmons, 1974; Weeks, 1930). In the 1940s these two states, then, must be judged as having moderately undemocratic voting systems for this reason.

VOTE DILUTION BY MALAPPORTIONMENT
AND GERRYMANDERING

Democratic theory assumes that once a person acquires the right to vote, his or her vote is equal in influence to that of any other single voter. Such has not always been the case in the United States because of the manner in which election districts have been drawn. The most typical problem here has been *malapportionment*. Some districts for the election of U.S. Congressmen, state legislators, or city council members, for example, may have many more qualified voters than others. Voters living in a less-populous district get proportionately more representation in such a situation because their district, despite having fewer voters, elects the same number of officeholders as do more populous districts. If such malapportionment assumes a systematic character—consistently favoring one sectional or political interest over another in a given state—then that interest is itself consistently better represented, too.

Gerrymandering, the deliberate manipulation of election district boundaries to favor one interest over another, has also been common in U.S. politics. It has been used, in particular, to limit the political influence of ethnic minority voters. A minority neighborhood, as an example, might be divided among several contiguous election districts, in none of which the minority voters would constitute a numerical majority. Hence, the minority voters' power would be diluted.

Malapportionment was virtually universal in the district boundaries for seats in state legislatures and in the U.S. House of Representatives in the 1940s. It assumed a systematic character that favored rural and small-town interests over those of large urban areas. This was the case partly because of the intense urbanization of the U.S. population during the twentieth century. In 1900 about 40 percent of Americans lived in what were urban areas according to U.S. Census Bureau definitions. By 1950 59 percent were urbanites. During the interval election district boundaries were seldom restructured to take account of the population shift. Hence, rural areas' political representation was far greater than was equitable based on their population.

Yet this malapportionment was not inevitable. The constitutions of many states called for periodic redrawing of district lines, often with population size being a principal criterion. Other states had carried out such reapportionment in earlier times by custom. But politicians with vested interests in the existing election arrangements typically refused to acknowledge this twentieth-century population shift. Many states did not reapportion their election districts at any time in the first half of this century. Others did so, but not in ways that fairly took account of the growing size of urban areas. And it was an explicit choice of political leaders that led to widespread malapportionment of this kind. As early as 1928 the writer and social critic H. L. Mencken observed of this situation, "The yokels hang on, because old apportionments give them unfair advantages."

Proving the existence of gerrymandering has been difficult outside the most blatant instances. In those regions where ethnic minorities could not vote at all or where other minority interests were historically underrepresented because of malapportionment, gerrymandering would not have been necessary. For these reasons there is no systematic documentation of the extent of gerrymandering on a state-by-state basis, and I cannot take account of it in my evaluations of the states. Yet we must recognize that this form of vote dilution was common in the 1940s.

Certain kinds of malapportionment, however, have been well-documented for that period, and the most common of these, as noted above, favored rural over urban political interests. In fact, such a bias was universal in the 1940s. It varied in magnitude across the states, but it was significant in all of them.

To estimate the degree of this problem, David and Eisenberg (1961: 14–16) calculated the relative values of the right to vote for state legislative representation in both the most and the least populous counties of each state after the 1930 and 1950 censuses (and after redistricting, if any, that followed those censuses). The 1930 figures do not take account of the continuing increase in urbanization through the 1930s and 1940s, and the 1950 figures underrepresent the degree of malapportionment in the 1940s in those states that redistricted after the 1950 census. Yet if we acknowledge these biases and use both figures to estimate the situation in the 1940s, all the states show notable malapportionment.

33

In the worst cases—in the states of Alabama, California, Florida, and Georgia—a single vote in the most populous counties was worth only *14–19* percent of a vote in the least populous counties in this period. Nationwide, a single vote in populous counties was worth about 55 percent of that in the most rural areas in the 1940s. Even in the most fairly apportioned states the relationship was no more than 65–80 percent after at least one of the two census years David and Eisenberg examined. When we compare these figures with the standard most typically enforced in contemporary apportionment lawsuits—that the populations of the smallest and the largest election districts should differ by no more than 1 percentage point (Bullock, 1982: 435)—it is fair to conclude that *all* the states exhibited notable vote dilution by malapportionment in the 1940s. Even greater vote dilution through gerrymandering and other forms of malapportionment existed in many of the other states, but it has not been systematically documented.

A Summary of Voting Rights in the 1940s

Drawing upon the preceding discussion, the states in the 1940s are rated here in the extent to which they had democratic suffrage laws. Table 2.2 provides a checklist of antidemocratic restrictions and suggests an ordinal scale by which to categorize the states in this regard. I emphasize that the first three columns of "moderate voting rights restrictions" concern less serious problems than those indicated under the fourth column: "extensive voting rights restrictions based on ethnicity." Thus a state's position on the overall scale of voting rights is indicated more by the nature of the problems indicated in the table than by the simple number of check marks it receives.

The 1940s "scores" of the states in Table 2.2 (and the comparable scores for the 1980s later in this chapter) indicate that we can divide the states among five possible ordinal categories according to the degree to which their voting rights were democratic. The full set of categories is (1) democratic, (2) polyarchic, (3) modestly undemocratic,

Table 2.2. Voting rights restrictions in the 1940s

State	Moderate Voting Rights Restrictions			Extensive Voting Rights Restrictions Based on Ethnicity
	Based on Malapportionment	By Political Machines	Based on Ethnicity or Literacy	
Alabama	X			X
Arizona	X		X	
Arkansas	X			X
California	X			
Colorado	X			
Connecticut	X			
Delaware	X			
Florida	X			X
Georgia	X			X
Idaho	X			
Illinois	X			
Indiana	X			
Iowa	X			

Table 2.2. Continued.

| | Moderate Voting Rights Restrictions | | | Extensive Voting Rights |
| | Based on Malappor-tionment | By Political Machines | Based on Ethnicity or Literacy | Restrictions Based on Ethnicity |
State				
Kansas	X			
Kentucky	X			
Louisiana	X			X
Maine	X			
Maryland	X			
Massachusetts	X			
Michigan	X			
Minnesota	X			
Mississippi	X			X
Missouri	X			
Montana	X			
Nebraska	X			
Nevada	X			
New Hampshire	X			
New Jersey	X			

State				
New Mexico	X		X	
New York	X			
North Carolina	X			X
North Dakota	X			
Ohio	X			
Oklahoma	X			
Oregon	X			
Pennsylvania	X			
Rhode Island	X			
South Carolina	X			X
South Dakota	X			
Tennessee	X			X
Texas	X			X
Utah	X	X		
Vermont	X			
Virginia	X	X		X
Washington	X			
West Virginia	X			
Wisconsin	X			
Wyoming	X			

(4) undemocratic, and (5) highly undemocratic. In the 1940s all forty-eight states fell into one of the three "undemocratic" categories. The groupings in the 1940s were

1. States with extensive voting rights limitations, which I label *highly undemocratic.* Alabama, Arkansas, Florida, Georgia, Louisiana, Mississippi, New Mexico, North Carolina, South Carolina, Tennessee, Texas, and Virginia constitute this group. While some might question whether New Mexico belongs in this category, I judge the obstacles to Native American and Mexican American voting rights in that state to have been sufficiently high that it be labeled highly undemocratic.

2. States where voting rights were limited by malapportionment and by either political machines or moderately restrictive ethnicity-based discrimination, which I label *undemocratic.* Arizona alone falls into this category.

3. States where voting rights were clearly limited by malapportionment and were doubtless often subject to gerrymandering and the activities of political machines, which I label *modestly undemocratic.* This category includes the remaining thirty-five states.

Some readers might wonder why the last category of states does not merit the label of polyarchies as defined in chapter 1. Three observations support the use of the more critical label of modestly undemocratic. First, the degree of malapportionment alone must be a significant qualification to the extent of democracy, as it seriously compromises the requirement for "popular equality" in a democracy (chap. 1). Second, machine politics and gerrymandering, which were common in many states in the 1940s, have not been sufficiently documented to be included in such a comparative evaluation. In other words, Table 2.2 *underestimates* the undemocratic voting and election practices actually operating in the 1940s. In the remainder of this chapter the discussions of the post-1940s evolution of voting rights in the United States, and of similar rights in other Western democracies, will more fully express what would be a truly democratic system of voting rights. The discussions will suggest another critical posture by which we must evaluate the suffrage laws of the 1940s.

The Voting Rights Revolution

By the 1980s a revolution in voting rights had occurred in the United States. Most of the legal restrictions on the suffrage had been swept away, and the potential electorate included virtually all adult citizens. The greatest beneficiaries of this change were ethnic minorities, but many others gained, too. Restrictions based on poll taxes, residence, literacy, native language, advance voter registration, and even barriers for the physically disabled have been eliminated or relaxed, making access to the ballot easier for all Americans.

More was transformed than just the prospective electorate: a new philosophy of suffrage rights lay behind these developments. Through the 1940s, voting required notable effort on the part of the individual citizen. Various barriers to registration were common. Many groups were effectively denied the right to vote—by their ethnicity, illiteracy, geographic mobility, inability to speak English, or limited income. The individual citizen had to take the initiative at every step along the way to the ballot box, and some of the hurdles in the path could be formidable. Many discussions of the right to vote at the time suggest that this was a good thing, as well.

Today our election laws are based on a radically different philosophy, one that calls for barriers to be low, voter effort to be limited, and responsibility for ensuring high turnout to be borne jointly by the government and the citizenry. Today residence and advance registration requirements are relatively short. Annual reregistration is a thing of the past in most states; merely voting periodically keeps one registered. State and federal governments actively sponsor voter registration drives, taking the initiative for citizens. Most minority-language voters can vote on a ballot in their own language, and handicapped and illiterate voters are assured assistance at the polls. Today the suffrage is seen not as a privilege that individuals must earn, but as a right that should be actively ensured by government.

There has been another change, too, and it accounts in good part for the preceding ones. The federal government has now assumed the greater responsibility for defining the right to vote. As discussed, the U.S. Constitution originally granted the states the power to define the suffrage. The federal government placed its first limits on state power in this area after the Civil War, but the Fourteenth and Fifteenth Amendments were only rights on paper for most African Americans for over one hundred years.

Indeed, in large part because of Southern resistance to African American voting, Uncle Sam eventually took most of the power to define the suffrage from the states. A series of federal court cases beginning in the 1940s and new laws beginning in the 1960s produced the change. The process took on a momentum that carried it far beyond African American suffrage, and the voting rights of many groups of Americans were affected in the process.

Despite near-universal suffrage, controversies remain, and our progress toward a fully democratic voting system is incomplete. Occasional violations of voting rights have been alleged, and often proven, in almost every state. In some states, resistance to minority political power and efforts to deny minority voting rights are still commonplace, not merely an occasional aspect of political life. Besides overt discrimination, a variety of other practices have arisen in some states to dilute minority voting power, as described under the topic of malapportionment. The vote dilution debate, protracted and far-reaching, has left philosophical, practical, and legal limits unsettled. Our system of voter registration is still somewhat undemocratic when compared with alternatives common in other Western nations.

To appreciate changes in the philosophy and reality of voting rights, we must briefly survey the principal legal changes that have occurred.

THE VOTING RIGHTS ACT

The Voting Rights Act of 1965, which was renewed and extended in 1970, 1975, and 1982, is the most important legal change in this area (Davidson, 1992). Originally aimed at the eleven ex-Confederate states and their disfranchisement of African Americans, it eventually was expanded to affect the entire nation. The original Voting Rights Act brought Southern states under direct federal government scrutiny with respect to their suffrage laws, suspended the use of literacy tests in most of those states, and provided for federal "voting examiners" who would supervise or actually carry out voter registration in these states when a federal court determined this procedure was necessary to overcome discriminatory practices. Those states covered under section 5 of the act also had to seek federal approval for any changes in their suffrage laws or in any other laws that might affect voting rights.[4]

The 1970 extension of the act brought more states under its coverage, mandated a residency requirement of no more than thirty days for voting in presidential elections, and lowered the voting age in such elections to eighteen.[5] In 1975 protection under the act was extended to Native Americans, Spanish Americans, Asian Americans, and Alaskan natives, and bilingual elections were required for these groups, depending on their number in a given jurisdiction and their literacy rate in English. All or parts of thirty-nine states were affected under either these provisions or the original ones directed at African Americans. The act also provided for challenges of voting restrictions in any state.

The provisions added in 1982 required that blind, disabled, and illiterate voters be allowed assistance at the polls.[6] The 1982 provisions also stipulated that voting rights violations need be proven only by their *results,* not by their *intent,* overturning a 1980 Supreme Court decision on this issue in *Mobile v. Bolden.* The requirement for federal approval of changes in state or local laws relating to voting rights was also extended for twenty-five years.

"ONE MAN, ONE VOTE"

The universal problem of malapportionment in legislative districts was ignored until the 1960s by legislatures themselves—many of the members of which benefited from the existing arrangements. Malapportionment was sidestepped also by the courts, as a "political," not a legal, question. Beginning in the 1960s, however, the U.S. Supreme Court agreed that malapportionment might violate the equality of voting rights implied, particularly, in the Fourteenth Amendment's provision for equal protection under the law.

In 1962 the court found this issue to be worthy of legal review in *Baker v. Carr,* returning the case to a lower court for a decision on its merits. In 1964 the Supreme Court itself ruled that seats in the U.S. House of Representatives must be districted according to equality of population (in *Wesberry v. Sanders*), and the Court set the same requirement for both houses of state legislatures (in *Reynolds v. Sims*). At the time, the standard invoked in these cases was dubbed "one man, one vote" (in the gender-neutral language of the 1990s, "one person, one vote").

The results of these cases were extraordinary. By 1970, for example, thirty-nine states had redistricted their U.S. House of Representatives seats on a "one person, one vote" basis, and after the 1970 census all House of Representatives and state legislative seats met this criterion. After each decennial census new apportionments must be crafted for these bodies in accordance with this standard.

THE DECLINE OF POLITICAL MACHINES

The machines are essentially gone, revived only in textbook discussions of urban politics for the sake of the vivid anecdotes and nasty criticism they can evoke. Chicago was the last machine-run big city, and vestiges of the organization remain there. But it is far weaker, less cohesive, and different in nature today than in its prime.

The machines were the victims of a number of forces. Muckrakers and reformers began to attack them at the turn of the century, scoring both their corruption and their inefficiency. Evolving public mores and tougher corruption laws have made machine-politics graft both politically and legally risky. Ferreting out bosses as well as politicians tied to machine organizations has also become a favorite sport of journalists—and of rival politicians.

To make the times even harder on machines, civil service and merit-employment schemes in government took away many of the jobs that had gone to ward-level minions. The welfare state replaced the machine as the provider of goods and services to the poor, and the struggle for minority civil rights in the 1960s produced challenges to the machines and their traditional leaders. Thus the sources of machine power and the reasons for voter loyalty have largely been stripped away. As far as manipulation of voters like that in the 1940s, the machines are dead.

THE POLITICS OF VOTING RIGHTS

In the wake of the Voting Rights Act and the "one person, one vote" standard, a political movement of equal importance arose to capitalize on these laws and ensure that their stated goals would be realized. A number of advocacy groups have taken on voting rights as a major concern. They have monitored state and local government compliance. They have sought legal relief from allegedly discriminatory practices—both in the courts and through the administrative mechanisms provided in the Voting Rights Act. And they have lobbied the Congress for the preservation and extension of the Voting Rights Act. The principal organizations active in this cause include the Legal Defense and Education Fund of the National Association for the Advancement of Colored People (NAACP), the Lawyers' Committee for Civil Rights Under Law, the Mexican American Legal Defense and Education Fund, the American Civil Liberties Union, the League of Women Voters, and the Southern Regional Council.

When the Voting Rights Act was passed in 1965, state and local elected officials from the South and southern members of Congress constituted the bulk of the opposing side. By the time of the 1982 extension, however, the numbers of vocal opponents to the act had declined precipitously. Even the majority of southern Congressmen voted for the extension. The political risks of opposition to this cause are too high for members of Congress who represent any appreciable number of minority constituents—precisely because their votes may be critical at election time.

In short, there has been a vigorous politics of voting rights since the early 1960s. That fact has kept this issue before the public, the Congress, and the president. It has generated considerable publicity for allegations of discrimination and for judicial and administrative actions to end discrimination. It has also extended the debate about voting rights to new concerns like vote dilution. Most important, however, the active politics surrounding this issue ensured that laws on the books would become laws in force. The political climate would not allow government to make a symbolic legal gesture and then ignore continued discrimination.

Perhaps activists in this area are stimulated, subconsciously at least, by recalling history. The Civil War supposedly led to a resolution of the voting rights issue, too. The Fourteenth and Fifteenth Amendments to the Constitution were adopted to guarantee African American civil rights. Yet, as noted, these laws were not enforced. Present-day voting rights activists do not want to see history repeated. Admittedly, they have been aided since the 1960s by greater public sympathy and by harmony between the branches of the federal government on this issue (at least at the most critical junctures). Yet if there is an urgency about the efforts of such activists, we might well understand it in light of history.

The revolution in voting rights since the 1940s has swept away patently undemocratic strictures, as well as many lesser barriers to the prospective voter. And a new philosophy of suffrage has begun to take shape, one where the initiative for the preservation and use of the right to vote lies as much with government as with the individual.

Voting Rights in the 1980s

Despite these remarkable advances, there remain some pockets of resistance and some distance yet to go toward a fully democratic system of suffrage. Efforts to restrict voting rights still arise occasionally in most states and quite frequently in others, albeit in a different form than in earlier days. And the concern with vote dilution, first raised in the "one person, one vote" cases with respect to simple population equality in representation, has taken on new and far more complex dimensions.

ACTIVE RESISTANCE TO MINORITY VOTING RIGHTS

We should not be surprised that there remains some resistance to the extension of civil rights. Many Americans were reared in a time when there was little respect for, even considerable discrimination against, ethnic minorities. Social mores prescribed that minorities were not the equals of the white population and were inferior in social and political position. Old values die hard, especially in those places where they have been most ingrained and carried to the greatest extremes. Anglo Americans with such attitudes still can be found across the nation, and instances of suffrage restriction can be found anywhere. The enforcement activities of the U.S. Department of Justice under the Voting Rights Act illustrate that such cases arise from time to time in many states.

The situation becomes critical, however, when efforts to circumscribe the suffrage are common, not just occasional, in any state. Frequent efforts of this kind indicate a systematic antidemocratic bias in the voting system. Unfortunately, there is considerable evidence that such efforts were still widespread in a handful of states in the 1980s. Indeed, they remain common in those states even today.

Evidence for this conclusion comes from a number of sources. First, in preparation for the debate in Congress about extension of the Voting Rights Act in 1982, the U.S. Commission on Civil Rights reviewed achievements under the act and compliance with its provisions. That review indicated that a variety of discriminatory election practices were still common in a few states. Those practices included (1) discrimination against individual minority citizens attempting to register to vote, (2) registration practices that systematically discriminated against minorities and the poor, (3) selective discrimination against individual minority citizens attempting to vote, (4) the manipulation of election procedures and locations so as to discriminate against minorities, (5) the manipulation of election district boundaries to dilute minority votes, (6) selective city annexations to dilute minority votes, (7) harassment of minority candidates for office, and (8) frequent avoidance of federal "preclearance" procedures in changing election practices that might have discriminatory effects (U.S. Commission on Civil Rights, 1981). The commission's report indicated that several of, if not all, these practices were common in Alabama, Georgia, Louisiana, Mississippi, North Carolina, South Carolina, and Texas.[7] A smaller, but still notable, number of discriminatory practices was observed in Virginia.

Second, a long stream of witnesses repeated and elaborated these allegations in hearings before a committee of the House of Representatives considering the extension of the Voting Rights Act in 1981. The three fat volumes of evidence from these hearings were instrumental in securing extension of the act by sizable majorities of both houses of Congress (Committee on the Judiciary, 1982). Further testimony on the continued existence of these voting restrictions was presented to the Congress in 1983 in additional hearings on the Voting Rights Act (Committee on the Judiciary, 1985).

The records of the U.S. Department of Justice's Civil Rights Division offer additional evidence of restrictive practices in these states. Between 1975 and 1981 remarkable numbers of election procedure changes proposed by Alabama, Georgia, Louisiana, Mississippi, North Carolina, South Carolina, and Texas were denied by the Civil Rights Division under the preclearance requirements of the Civil Rights Act (U.S. Commission on Civil Rights, 1981: 68; Committee on the Judiciary, Part 3, 1982: 2231–42). This fact, coupled with the observation that many other such changes were never submitted to the Civil Rights Division for review, or were submitted only after pressure by the Department of Justice or litigation by outside parties, underscores the frequency of efforts to abridge voting rights in these states. Recent reports by the Civil Rights Division indicate that there is still a remarkable number of such obstructions in these states (Committee on Appropriations, 1987: 556–57, 565–66).[8]

Further, evidence of bias against minority political influence in these states comes from their legislative reapportionments after the 1980 census. The original apportionment plans prepared by state officials in Georgia, Louisiana, Mississippi, North Carolina, and Texas were overturned by the U.S. Department of Justice or by federal courts for minority vote dilution or racial gerrymandering.[9] In addition, a federal court itself drew the districting plan in South Carolina in response to an NAACP legal suit over racial vote dilution. Alabama's districting plans were challenged on similar grounds by local minorities but were accepted by the Department of Justice (*Congressional Quarterly,* 1983). In other words, voting rights are occasionally at risk in isolated instances in most states, but there is evidence of systematic efforts to infringe such rights in Alabama, Georgia, Louisiana, Mississippi, North Carolina, South Carolina, and Texas.

THE NEW FACE OF VOTE DILUTION

When the U.S. Supreme Court issued its "one person, one vote" edict in the mid-1960s, the underlying conception of vote dilution seemed clear, easy to document, and easy to reverse. Simple equality of population in election districts was the legal expectation. But the value of ethnic minority votes may be diminished by a variety of election practices beyond population imbalance, as when some state or local governments sought to change their election procedures to avoid the obvious consequences of minority enfranchisement under the

Voting Rights Act. Some tried to change from district to at-large elections, for example. In such cases a minority group that would otherwise have constituted the majority of a single district—and hence could have elected a minority representative—was instead submerged within the larger community and its Anglo majority. Election district gerrymandering, the annexation by cities of areas with large Anglo populations to diminish the proportion of minorities in the jurisdiction, and a variety of other maneuvers might have the same ultimate effect (Davidson, 1984). Beyond such evasions, many election procedures that operated to dilute minority votes had been in place long before the Voting Rights Act and, hence, might not be challenged under that law.

At first, the elimination of new forms of vote dilution appeared easy: simply ban the offending election procedure. Yet a host of questions complicate that seemingly easy solution (Grofman, Handley, and Niemi, 1992). Proving the discriminatory result alone can be difficult. The right to vote is not denied by these procedures, only the value of the vote. Because vote dilution can arise through a variety of "subtle practices," as they are known in the literature on this subject, and because it is widely acknowledged that vote dilution itself is difficult to define and prove, legal grounds for eradicating such practices have been equally difficult to fashion. The Congress added language to the Voting Rights Act in 1982 that is directed at this problem (Derfner, 1984), but this revision does not even provide a clear definition of vote dilution. Nor has the Supreme Court found a consistent standard of proof or interpretation for cases in this area. The Court established a three-part test for vote dilution in 1986 in the case *Thornburg v. Gingles*. Yet there remain notable ambiguities about this test and about how it applies to many specific cases of alleged dilution (Grofman, Handley, and Niemi, 1992: 29–81; Jacobs and O'Rourke, 1986).

Remedies for vote dilution have been equally elusive and controversial. If, for example, it is decided that there should be district or ward elections instead of the at-large type, how should the election districts be drawn? Should minorities be heavily concentrated in single districts to ensure the election of a single minority representative? Or should their numbers be dispersed to give many candidates a reason to respond to their interests? And what is the logical end to which these concerns point? Some argue that only proportional representation of separate minority groups would satisfy the new concerns about vote dilution. These questions remain controversial, and there are both conservative positions (Blumstein, 1983; O'Rourke, 1992; Thernstrom, 1987) and liberal stances (Davidson, 1984; Grofman and Davidson, 1992) on how to answer them.

Election laws and practices that might dilute minority voting strength can be found across the nation. Only in a handful of southern states, however, is there evidence that these laws have commonly been manipulated in deliberate attempts to reduce minority political power; the extent of democracy in Alabama, Georgia, Louisiana, Mississippi, North Carolina, South Carolina, and Texas must be further qualified because of the existence of such practices.

REGISTRATION SYSTEM BARRIERS TO VOTING

It has long been widely recognized that voting turnout in the entire United States is remarkably lower than that in most other Western democracies. The explanations have been widely debated, too, and the hypothesized villains include voter apathy, the nature of the U.S. political party system, and restrictive voter registration and election laws. Recent research has indicated that the legal restrictions, despite the relaxation discussed here, are still especially important (see, as examples, Glass et al., 1984; Jackman, 1987; Powell, 1986).

In almost every other Western democracy the burden of voter registration is borne almost entirely by the government, typically by way of a systematic, periodic canvas of the entire population. In other countries where voters must initiate the registration process themselves, they are often required to do so by law. Many countries further encourage voting by holding elections on weekends or by designating election days as holidays. Several countries even have financial or other penalties for failure to vote (Powell, 1980: 9–10).

In contrast, U.S. laws still leave the principal burden on the citizen, in spite of the progress we have made toward governmental responsibility. Our election laws thus pose notable barriers to registration and voting in comparison with those of most other democratic nations. Powell (1986) estimates that our registration laws alone may reduce turnout in national elections by as much as 14 percent of the voting-age population when compared with the "automatic" registration systems of other countries. And Glass et al. (1984: 53) observe that even those U.S. states with the least restrictive registration laws— those allowing election-day sign-up—have various other impediments that go beyond automatic registration systems. Only North Dakota requires no voter registration. The suffrage and election laws of the remaining forty-nine states pose notable impediments to the right to vote, not only according to the abstract, highly demanding ideal of perfect democracy but also in terms of the actual performance of a number of other nations.

A Summary of Voting Rights in the 1980s

Based on the preceding survey of voting rights in the 1980s, we can divide the states into three groups. North Dakota alone deserves a *democratic* rating, in large measure for the openness of its voter registration system.

The seven southern states with continuing and systematic, if subtle, attacks on minority voting—Alabama, Georgia, Louisiana, Mississippi, North Carolina, South Carolina, and Texas—should be judged *moderately undemocratic,* in keeping with the criteria employed for the comparable evaluations for the 1940s. In these states the various voting rights restrictions are but separate aspects of a broad resistance to minority rights. They might thus be thought of as a single kind of

50

voting limitation. The restrictions take a number of forms, however, as the debate over the Voting Rights Act extension in 1982 revealed, and their multifaceted nature is testimony to their seriousness.

The remaining forty-two states merit a *polyarchic* rating under the criteria employed here. Voting rights are substantially assured in these states, but isolated instances of restriction still arise in many of them. In addition, suffrage is determined in all of them by election laws and practices that are to some degree restrictive when compared with those of other Western nations.

Conclusions

Voting rights have indeed been revolutionized in the second half of the twentieth century. At midcentury the suffrage was significantly abridged in almost a third of the states. In the ex-Confederate states the limits were so severe as to make it ludicrous to call those states democratic. In all the states in the 1940s vote dilution significantly qualified this most basic of political rights.

By the 1980s only a handful of states still exhibited notable restrictions. Achieving near-universal suffrage is certainly remarkable, but it does not diminish the importance of the remaining laggard states. Admittedly, an extensive legal and administrative apparatus exists today to assist those whose right to vote has been wrongly abridged. Yet a frank assessment of the prospects would be that this right will not be fully secure across the South for another generation. As observed earlier, centuries-old social mores die slowly.

After reading the history of the voting rights controversy, evaluating its course, and considering, as well, the comments of a number of observers in the two periods under consideration, I am left with one more striking observation. Near-universal suffrage in the United States was achieved in good part because it became an issue of community in the 1950s and 1960s. As late as the 1940s it was widely recognized that many Americans were denied the right to vote and other civil rights, but there was little national concern or indignation about such injustice. Most of the crusaders at the time were African Americans, Native Americans, and Mexican Americans—those who themselves suffered limitations on their political and social rights. Even the crusaders, however, were a surprisingly temperate lot in the 1940s, and they were definitely but a modest minority of Americans. It was not until the 1960s that voting rights infringement was widely recognized as a stain on the national democratic record or a violation of the sense of national community. By the 1960s a new, more thoroughly democratic sense of political community began to evolve. Through this change in public philosophy, two hundred years after Madison wrote the dictum defining the political community, it was largely realized.

3

Political Party Competition

In every free and deliberating society, there must, from the nature of man, be opposite parties, and violent dissensions and discords; and one of these, for the most part, must prevail over the other for a longer or shorter time.

Thomas Jefferson

Effective competition between rival political views is central to democracy. In large modern societies, however, this requirement takes on a special character, demanding mechanisms that can overcome the practical obstacles: dispersion of and limited communication among those who hold the same political preferences. Societies need institutions that can sweep together like-minded individuals and demonstrate both their numbers and their political interests.

Political parties have traditionally been seen as the most efficacious vehicles for carrying out this task. Indeed, some have argued that parties are essential here. As E. E. Schattschneider (1942: 1), a leading proponent of this view, says, "The political parties created democracy and modern democracy is unthinkable save in terms of parties." Other students of parties echo this sentiment (for example, Burnham, 1982; Key, 1956; and Ranney and Kendall, 1956). Still others might say that parties are quite useful, if not essential, in this role (Ware, 1987).

All observers agree that political parties perform several specific tasks related to this broad purpose. They provide institutional bases around which like-minded citizens can rally in an effort to influence government. They recruit candidates who run for office under the banner and in the interests of the party. They publicize the party's views to all voters to gain additional support. And those candidates who are elected to office from a given party can pursue their common political goals within the government. Much as this list may sound like civics text pablum, such activities are critical.

Organizing elections, recruiting candidates, and publicizing issues are political activities that we would not want the government itself to perform, but they must be carried out if democracy is to exist in any degree. Parties arose early in U.S. history precisely to fill these and related functions. Similarly, when a majority party takes the reins of government, it takes up what is in a sense a neutral set of institutions that might otherwise know no particular direction or goals. Or, worse than being neutral, the government might follow its own goals. Parties bring life and direction to government.

In a general sense, then, parties fulfill a *linkage* function; they are mechanisms for communication whereby public sentiments are transmitted to government. Behind the day-to-day and election-to-election activities is this broader purpose. In large mass societies, in particular, parties are the most effective institutions for aggregating and transmitting public preferences, thereby overcoming the practical obstacles in the way of expressing the majority will.

But there is another dimension to this role, too: *competition* between parties, which is considered essential for democracy. Jefferson's observation about the inevitability of political differences is widely shared. Yet those differing points of view require organizational expression to be fairly represented in the governing process. Without that representation and, hence, that competition, important political views are sure to be ignored by government. This assumption is so commonplace that it is made without comment or explanation in much of the traditional scholarship on parties and democracy.

Parties have always filled these roles in some measure in the United States. My present task is to demonstrate the extent to which they did so in each of the fifty states in the 1940s and the 1980s. First of all we must recognize some of the limits on the linkage role and some of the implications of party competition.

The communication function described by the term linkage does not necessarily imply a neutral translation of majority sentiment into public policy, or even into party program. Democratic theory envisions such a direct result as the ideal. Students of everyday politics, however, recognize that only humbler forms of linkage actually exist, and they disagree about how close these are to the democratic standard. By considering some of the critical perspectives on parties we can explore some of the reasons for that disagreement.

One especially critical view is that party competition and the election process allow citizens to choose their leaders, but not government policies. A prominent, and pessimistic, version of this view is that of Schumpeter (1942: 250–68) who argues that average voters are incapable of expressing rational or meaningful choices about government policies (262):

> The typical citizen drops down to a lower level of mental performance as soon as he enters the political field. He argues and analyzes in a way he would readily recognize as infantile within the sphere of his real interests. He becomes a primitive again. His thinking becomes associative and affective.

Schumpeter goes on to argue that the true role of citizens in a democracy is to choose government leaders through elections. Once installed in office, these leaders have wide discretion in selecting government policies, but that discretion is ultimately constrained because of competition from prospective government leaders. Schumpeter (1942: 280) sees this competition as "the essence of democracy."

55

Another critical argument about the limits of democratic linkage is based on the view that U.S. political parties are not "parties of principle." They are more concerned with seeking public offices than with achieving policy programs. Lowi (1975), for example, argues that U.S. parties have been principally concerned with the former goal from the time of their creation. Other scholarship has articulated further the theory that parties and candidates are principally concerned with getting elected and remaining in office (Fiorina, 1977; Mayhew, 1974). If we expect organizations that indeed have such goals to carry on direct and detailed communication about policy with the electorate, we misunderstand their character. At the same time Lowi recognizes the importance of competition among parties for the maintenance of democracy, even if the object is only the right to control government offices. "For the functioning of party itself, the important fact has been the existence of competition, not so much what the competition was about" (Lowi, 1975: 255).

Still another prominent view is that competitive elections allow only *retrospective,* generalized evaluation of the incumbent party and administration (Fiorina, 1981). Future policy is not prescribed by voters making choices among candidates, according to this thesis. Instead, the election-time evaluation of candidates and parties is based principally on reactions to the record of the incumbents. That evaluation may also be sweeping and highly generalized instead of clearly associated with particular policy efforts. Thus only a kind of broad-gauged, after-the-fact public control of parties and candidates exists in this view. Nonetheless, the process allows a measure of public control, and it establishes some expectations for public officials in terms of that control. And the existence of a competitive "out party" gives force and urgency to the "in-party's" concern for the public's retrospective evaluations in the future.

Thus there are several critical theoretical views of the degree and character of public influence over government through parties. Yet even these critics readily agree as to the perils of an absence of competition. Students of one-party nations abroad (Palmer and Thompson, 1978: 223–59) and of one-party states at home (Key, 1949; Miller, 1956) have provided ample empirical evidence for this conclusion. Research on both national and state political processes offers additional evidence of the centrality of party competition for public control over government policy (Hurley, 1989b; Erikson et al., 1989). Thus some scholars may be skeptical about the degree of linkage arising out of parties and election processes, but they agree on the importance of competition among parties.

Contrary to these critical theoretical views of parties, however, there is considerable empirical evidence that U.S. parties do carry out policy linkage functions. Both classic and contemporary research has demonstrated that the two major *national* parties are indeed ideologically different (McClosky et al., 1960; Hurley, 1989a). The national parties adopt platforms that reflect those differences (Monroe, 1983), and their representatives in government generally pursue the goals set out in those platforms (Pomper and Lederman, 1980). Recent research on *state* politics has also demonstrated important linkage processes. In particular, Erikson et al. (1989) have shown that state parties respond to the ideological preferences of state electorates and that elections reward those parties that do so most successfully. And there is evidence in both national and state politics of considerable convergence between public preferences and government policies (Monroe, 1979; Page and Shapiro, 1983; Wright et al., 1987).

Doubtless, public influence over government is higher in a direct democracy like that of the Greek city-states discussed in chapter 1 (recalling the qualification, of course, of the limited right to participate in such governments in the first place). Representative government systems are inevitably more circumscribed in this respect, but even so they allow real democratic possibilities. And the extent to which they do so is dependent, in part, on effective competition between alternative views about appropriate government policy. Without that competition, principally in the form of contests between political parties, we fail to approximate democracy.

Party Competition in the States before the 1940s

Political parties did not exist at the time of the founding of our nation, but they developed fairly quickly during its early years (Chambers, 1963). In fact, modern political parties in Western nations were a U.S. invention. Between the 1830s and the abolitionist conflict of the 1850s and 1860s, the two major parties competed on generally equal footing within most individual states. There existed, that is, widespread two-party competition (Ladd, 1970: 100–103).

The conflict over slavery and the Civil War, however, set in motion a number of political changes that resulted in considerable deterioration in this competitiveness. After the war the former Confederate states and a few Border states became solidly Democratic—because of the sentiments of their residents concerning the war and the positions of the two parties on the war and on the slavery question. Similarly, one-party Republicanism characterized a number of New England, midwestern, and western states.

The political conflicts that arose early in the period of industrialization in the late nineteenth century exacerbated the trend toward one-partyism and sectionally divided politics. These conflicts pitted the interests of the largely agrarian South and parts of the West against those of the industrializing Northeast and Midwest. Thus the agrarian base of the Democratic party was enhanced, as was the urban and industrial base of the Republicans. At the same time there were declines in both parties' ability to compete on the other's turf.

The resulting pattern of partisan alignments characterized the period 1890–1930. Ladd (1970: 175–76), for example, categorizes only twenty-one of the forty-eight states as two-party competitive in presidential elections between 1892 and 1928. For about the same period Burnham (1981: 176–81) identifies nineteen one-party Republican and fourteen one-party Democratic states in terms of control of the state legislatures.

Most observers argue, however, that two-party competition has increased substantially in the states since 1930. Two explanations have been advanced for why such a change might be inevitable. First, other political issues have taken the place of the motivations for one-partyism arising from the Civil War and the debate over industrial policy in the 1890s. The old reasons for which people were loyal to one party or another have declined in importance, and new issues have divided the parties and the electorate in new ways.

Second, it has been argued that economic and social development within states would lead to two-party competition where it had not existed before. Increased industrialization, urbanization, and related forms of "modernization" should, that is, lead to a greater diversity of political interests and conflicts, which could not be contained within the old single-party systems (Morehouse, 1981: 58–60). Two or even more parties might be necessary to represent all these diverse political interests.

In sum, one-party domination of individual states has been more the rule than the exception through U.S. history—in spite of our longstanding rhetoric that this is a two-party nation and the appearance, at least, of two-party competition at the national level, given the results of all the one-party contests across the nation. At the same time there were good reasons to expect a general increase in party competitiveness in the second half of the twentieth century. But what, in fact, has been the record in this period?

Party Competition in State Politics in the 1940s and 1980s

To assess levels of party competition in the states, I have relied on a measure originated by Ranney (1965), which has become the standard yardstick for such competition. The index focuses on major party competition for control of the governorship and the state legislature. It takes account of (1) the degree of success by one party, as

59

indicated by the percentage of gubernatorial votes or legislative seats won by the party; (2) the duration of time that a single party controls the legislature and the governorship; and (3) the consequent frequency of divided party control. For the purposes of this book, the measure was calculated for the periods 1946–52 and 1980–86.[1]

For each period the calculation results in an index indicating the extent of Democratic versus Republican control of state institutions: a score of 0 indicates Republican control of all legislative seats and all gubernatorial votes, and a score of 100 indicates similarly complete Democratic control. Based on criteria originated by Ranney (1965) and modified by Tucker (1982), the index is used to divide the states into three categories: one-party domination, two-party competition, and modified or weak one-party control.

Tables 3.1 and 3.2 present the individual state scores and the categorizations by type of competition for the two periods. In the 1940s only thirteen states merited the designation "two-party competitive" by this measure. In these states changes of party control of both the governorship and the individual houses of the legislature were common. Both parties typically also had quite respectable numbers of legislative seats during this period. The parties competed, then, on essentially equal footing. The out-party was a credible threat to the in-party, constituting an effective opposition in day-to-day policy-making and presenting a competitive challenge at elections.

Fourteen states were solidly one-party, most of them former Confederate states still under the banner of the Democrats. The extent of single party domination in all fourteen one-party states was quite remarkable. In the most extreme cases the opposition party did not hold a single seat in the legislature and at times did not even run a candidate for the governorship. In these one-party states, whether Republican or Democratic, it would be charitable to say the second party had even token influence in state government.

Twenty-one states are categorized as having modified or weak one-party government in the 1940s. In practical terms the second

Table 3.1. Party competition in state politics in the 1940s

One-Party Democratic	Modified Democratic	Two-Party Competitive	Modified Republican	One-Party Republican
Georgia (100)	Arizona (80)	Rhode Island (59)	Indiana (37)	South Dakota (15)
Louisiana (100)	Oklahoma (80)	Missouri (56)	Idaho (36)	Vermont (12)
Mississippi (100)	Kentucky (75)	Utah (51)	Michigan (36)	North Dakota (9)
South Carolina (100)	West Virginia (73)	Nevada (50)	Ohio (34)	
Texas (98)	New Mexico (71)	Washington (47)	Wyoming (34)	
Alabama (97)	Maryland (70)	Massachusetts (46)	New York (31)	
Arkansas (96)		Minnesota (42)	Pennsylvania (29)	
Florida (95)		Delaware (41)	New Hampshire (25)	
North Carolina (90)		Montana (41)	New Jersey (25)	
Virginia (89)		Nebraska (40)	California (23)	
Tennessee (87)		Colorado (39)	Wisconsin (20)	
		Connecticut (39)	Iowa (19)	
		Illinois (39)	Oregon (19)	
			Kansas (18)	
			Maine (16)	

Table 3.2. Party competition in state politics in the 1980s

One-Party Democratic	Modified Democratic	Two-Party Competitive	Modified Republican	One-Party Republican
Maryland (90)	Alabama (83)	New Mexico (62)	Colorado (37)	
Mississippi (87)	Arkansas (83)	Connecticut (61)	Wyoming (36)	
Georgia (86)	Kentucky (83)	Maine (61)	Arizona (35)	
	Louisiana (83)	Ohio (60)	Kansas (33)	
	Massachusetts (82)	Illinois (56)	New Hampshire (32)	
	South Carolina (81)	New York (55)	Idaho (31)	
	Hawaii (79)	Washington (54)	Indiana (30)	
	North Carolina (77)	Alaska (53)	Utah (26)	
	West Virginia (77)	Montana (53)	South Dakota (23)	
	Rhode Island (76)	New Jersey (53)		
	Virginia (75)	Delaware (51)		
	Oklahoma (74)	Iowa (50)		
	Florida (73)	Nebraska (49)		
	Texas (73)	Vermont (41)		
	Nevada (70)	Pennsylvania (40)		
	Wisconsin (68)	North Dakota (38)		
	Missouri (67)			
	Tennessee (67)			
	Michigan (66)			
	California (65)			
	Oregon (65)			
	Minnesota (64)			

Table 3.3. Party competition summary

Measure of Competition	1940s	1980s
Number of states with		
One-party systems	14	3
One-party-dominant systems	21	31
Two-party systems	13	16
Average competitiveness	25	18
Average Democratic-ness	53	60

party had sizable minority strength in the legislature and even won occasional gubernatorial contests in many of these states. The second party could not hope to control the government fully, but it was a credible opposition in certain limited respects.

As observed above, there were plausible reasons to believe that party competition would increase between the 1940s and the 1980s, and that the increase would then be revealed in a comparison of the two tables. Yet the actual results provide only modest support for those expectations. The number of one-party states did decline precipitously, to only three in the 1980s, but those meriting the two-party label rose only from thirteen to sixteen. Table 3.2 shows that the greatest movement has been into the modified or weak Democratic party column. In particular, moderate but notable erosion of the formerly one-party systems in the South shifted many of the states of the region into this column. But states from other areas around the nation have moved into this category since the 1940s, as well.

To summarize these results empirically, table 3.3 lists the number of states in each category of competition in each period, along with two additional measures of competition. The "average Democratic-ness" score is simply the average of the individual state scores in the previous tables. In the 1940s the states were fairly evenly divided between the Republican-leaning and the Democratic-leaning—as indicated by the average near the midpoint of 50 on this measure. The numerical increase in this average by the 1980s reflects the general movement of states toward Democratic control.

The "average competitiveness" score is calculated by eliminating the partisan component from the scores in the prior tables. That is, the original 0 to 100 scale is folded at 50, and states are given new scores that indicate their distance from this midpoint of perfectly equal competitiveness (regardless of whether they diverge from it in a Republican or a Democratic direction). Henceforth, I will use this new measure as my indicator of the degree of party competition in each of the states. The decline in the numeric value of the latter index between the 1940s and the 1980s indicates some overall improvement in competitiveness across the states. That is, the average state moved somewhat closer to the endpoint on the scale representing equal competitiveness, but the other results in this table indicate the limited scope of this movement.

Based on the preceding results and their practical meaning for politics within states, I conclude that states with two-party competition are *democratic.* One-party states must be labeled *highly undemocratic,* while modified one-party states merit the designation of *polyarchies.* Thus these results support both positive and not-so-positive conclusions. The number of one-party, hence undemocratic, party systems has been dramatically reduced, but two-party competition in state politics is virtually no more common today than in the 1940s. Admittedly, in many states there is moderate competitiveness today where there was little or none in the earlier time, but democratic party systems still exist in only about one-third of the states.

Party Competition in National versus State Politics
The results in the preceding tables may be surprising for some readers who are familiar with the support that recent U.S. presidential can-

Table 3.4. Average vote for Democratic presidential candidates by party control of state politics (as percentages of those voting)

	Party Control of State Political Institutions				
Period	One-Party Democratic	Modified Democratic	Two-Party	Modified Republican	One-Party Republican
1940s	61	52	48	44	37
1980s	47	44	41	33	—

didates have received in particular states. Presidential elections suggest very different patterns of partisanship and competitiveness. Most notably, in many of the states shown to be controlled by the Democrats in these tables, Republican presidential candidates have been quite successful in recent elections. This fact illustrates what some might see as an odd pattern—the seeming isolation of state-level partisanship from that in national elections.

Table 3.4 presents evidence on the relationship in party success between these two levels of elections. The average vote for Democratic presidential candidates is shown for each category of Democratic versus Republican control of state politics derived from the earlier tables.[2] In both time periods the pattern of Democratic presidential success across the state-party control categories indicates there is convergence in the expected direction. In other words, Democratic presidential candidates are more successful in states with greater Democratic control of state politics. The relationship was far stronger, however, in the 1940s. In that period Democratic presidential contenders won more Democratic states on average and split the vote in two-party states. Similarly, Republican presidential contenders won on average in Republican states. In effect, then, there was little disparity between partisanship in state versus national elections in the 1940s.

In the portion of the 1980s encompassed in this research Republican Ronald Reagan won a majority of presidential votes in all four categories of states. Thus there was a remarkable divide between state- and presidential-level partisanship by this time. Some might believe the early 1980s to be an unrepresentative period, with greater than usual Republican success in national politics, but virtually every Republican presidential candidate since Dwight Eisenhower has gotten strong voter support nationwide. It is admittedly the case that presidential votes overstate Republican success in national politics, because Democrats have controlled both houses of Congress by notable majorities through most of the period after World War II. Nonetheless, the results in table 3.4 testify to the divergence of party success across different elections and levels of government.

The roots of this pattern of divergence lie, in part, in the regional schism in the Democratic party and the ideological and issue basis for that schism. In the Northeast and selected other areas Democrats are relatively liberal. In the South, of course, they are relatively conservative. The two wings of the party were joined successfully for a time during the administration of President Franklin Roosevelt, but subsequent Democratic presidential nominees have been less successful in maintaining that unity and in fashioning national election majorities. Thus the results in table 3.4 for the 1980s are in part a product of the desire of the Southern electorate to support conservative candidates in most elections. To do so, however, they have typically voted for Democrats at home and Republicans in the White House. In other regions of the nation, similar kinds of voter sentiment may have also produced a divergence of partisanship across elections.

The partisanship of individual voters in national elections does, in fact, filter down to state contests, but that filtering process is a slow and imperfect one. Southern states, as an example, were giving notable support to Republican presidential candidates in the early

1950s. Yet Southern voters' support for Republican candidates in state and local elections rose far more slowly. Likewise, Southern politicians were slow to enter the Republican party and to engage in the hard task of building a competitive second party.

Over time, these slow processes have accumulated in their effects and have enhanced the competitiveness of state politics in the South, and the "modernization" of that region has helped the process. The region is far more complex economically and socially today than in the 1940s. Migration to the South from other regions brought many new voters with Republican loyalties. And the enfranchisement of Southern blacks made state politics more divisive. All these changes have made the politics of the South more complicated and less susceptible to one-party control. Despite that fact, despite the enormity of these social and political changes, and despite the attractiveness of Republican presidential candidates in the region, effective party competition in state politics has evolved slowly.

Nationwide, patterns of state party system evolution have been more variable. While the South has become more Republican and, hence, more competitive, some other states have become more Democratic and, sometimes, less competitive. This phenomenon is remarkable, too, for it is contrary to the nationwide trend of Republican success in presidential races. The late 1970s saw increased Democratic success in a number of state political races, and many observers attributed this change to disillusionment with the Republican party after the Watergate episode and the resignation of President Richard Nixon. But the early 1980s—the period of President Reagan's enormous personal popularity and of the notable policy successes early in his administration—witnessed only modest Republican gains in state and local races. And Democrats erased many of those gains and strengthened their control in a number of states in 1986 and 1988.

Overall, these observations suggest that party competitiveness in state elections evolves, in part, for reasons distinctive from those that affect national politics. The two levels are doubtless related, but the relationship is mediated by complex state-level forces that foreclose an easy prediction of one pattern from the other. Thus it is not inevitable that two-party competition, or any other pattern that predominates in national politics, will eventually permeate state politics.

Impediments to the Growth of Two-Party Competition

The slow development of competitive politics is explained by several related reasons. In some states traditional voter loyalties to a particular party may be strong and widely shared, allowing that party to dominate politics in the state. Those loyalties may be rooted in momentous historical events in which the party played a role, or they may simply result from the long prominence of a given party in a state. Residents of such states are socialized to identify with that party, and that socialization is the product of family, peer, and institutional influences. Mere custom becomes a powerful source of party strength in such areas.

Dominant parties often enjoy an ideological advantage, as well, the result of traditional voters' policy preferences. Some states, that is, are relatively conservative, and some are relatively liberal. If there is a dominant party in such states, it has customarily occupied the ideological "center of gravity" of the state. A newly emerging second party is faced with a dilemma in this situation. It may attempt to draw together the excluded interests, but they may not be numerous enough to fashion electoral majorities. The only alternative, then, is to challenge the dominant party for the support of its traditional supporters. The circumstances that Republicans face in the South offer a good example of the difficulties of the latter strategy. Southern Democrats occupy the conservative ideological ground that is the natural position of Republicans elsewhere. Thus Republicans cannot easily write off their opponents as "nasty liberals" and then proceed to take their own customary policy posture. Instead Republicans must fashion different campaign strategies by offering themselves as "better" conservatives or as more competent candidates, and the latter claims are often difficult to justify.

Dominant parties have many other advantages. Because of their historical prominence, such parties can more easily attract ambitious, would-be politicians. Some aspirants join the dominant party out of traditional loyalties just like those of many voters. But some do so for strategic reasons. They are more likely to be successful in seeking office under the banner of the dominant party than under that of the minority one.

The ability to recruit a large pool of candidates is important in several ways. We think most readily of its implications for the most prominent state offices—the governorship and other state executive branch offices. Fielding attractive candidates for these races at the top of the ticket is a critical first requirement for any party. But the lower-level races are critical, as well. Many an emerging second party has found itself able to run a successful candidate for governor, and the party faithful are elated by the seeming triumph on election day. But when many of those governors, once in office, begin to fashion their executive and policy programs, they realize they have few co-partisans in other executive offices or in the legislature to assist in that effort. The other offices are still largely monopolized by members of the dominant party. Thus emerging minority parties often have a difficult time in demonstrating, while holding office, what they can actually achieve, and their inability to field a full slate of attractive candidates at elections is one reason for this difficulty.

Traditional voter loyalties to the dominant party have an important influence on this problem for the minority party. In prominent, well-publicized races, voters may know both candidates relatively well, and choices between the two can be influenced by a candidate's style, personality, positions on issues, and campaign strategy. Thus minor-party gubernatorial candidates are sometimes successful in a number of states in spite of the weakness of their general partisan support. In lower-level races, voters typically know much less about candidates and have few cues besides their party upon which to base a choice. The races are not as well publicized, campaign expenditures are more modest, and neither the personalities nor the issue positions of the candidates are well known. It is easy in the latter situation for the voter to fall back upon his or her traditional party preference in selecting among candidates. In one-party or dominant-party states this behavior results, of course, in a strong bias in favor of the majority party. This behavior becomes unduly important because only a handful of election races are typically well-publicized or otherwise controversial. Even state legislative races may be obscure affairs for many voters. The incumbent—who likely is a member of the dominant party in one-party states—will be recognized at least by name. If the challenger is dimly perceived, the choice can become automatic, based on personal partisan loyalty.

Dominant parties and their candidates are also typically more successful in raising funds for election campaigns. Their past election successes make them more attractive—better risks—for those who use campaign contributions to ensure access to elected officials. Naturally, with better campaign funding these parties can better advertise their candidates and, in the process, reinforce voters' acquaintance with the candidates for whose party they already have a traditional loyalty.

Dominant parties enjoy one other power: they can often manipulate election laws to their benefit. The most obvious and traditional way of doing this is by gerrymandering election district boundaries for partisan advantages (see chap. 2). For most of this century dominant state parties did this as a matter of custom, or they avoided redrawing election boundaries entirely if failing to do so would produce the desired partisan results. Even today, under the legal dictum of "one person, one vote," dominant parties enjoy this power to some degree. State legislatures typically draw up or ultimately select the plan for new congressional and state legislative districts after each decennial census, and it has been widely alleged that partisan motives are common in such plans. Equal-population districts can often be constructed to ensure any of a variety of partisan outcomes; it is not surprising that the leaders of dominant parties seek to ensure their own fortunes in this manner. And many observers argue that state regulations concerning party organizations, campaign finance, and elections inhibit the development of smaller parties.[3]

Dominant parties thus enjoy several opportunities by which they can sustain their position in state politics. When wisely employed, these opportunities have simultaneous and reinforcing influence to that end. One of their consequences is to diminish the influence of national political events on competitiveness at state and local levels. Another may be to slow the supposedly "natural" growth of competitiveness arising from socioeconomic development.

Conclusions

If opposing parties are in the nature of man, as Jefferson said, then certain features of most state political systems have prevented the realization of such political oppositions. Only a minority of states enjoy effective two-party competition today; movement in that direction in other states has been limited; and there is little evidence to suggest notable progress in the near future. Institutional political forces, and perhaps a measure of mass political inertia, operate to retard such developments. Hence, the levels of party competition in the states today may be with us for some time.

4

Participation in Elections

I don't vote, but what I got to vote for?
African American woman in Georgia, 1939

Public participation in government is the trait most commonly associated with democracy. To most people it is the practical expression of government "by the people." Yet opportunities for participation are affected by the size of both the nation and the government. As discussed in chapter 1, participation in government in large modern nations is inevitably more circumscribed than was the case in either ancient Greek or New England town meeting democracies.

Of necessity, then, elections take on special importance in large polities. Elections offer the only occasions where the majority of citizens can participate in government affairs *and* make a collective decision in the process. Other opportunities for expressing concerns to government exist, as do some means for more extensive involvement in actual policy decisions. But relatively few citizens take advantage of these opportunities, and thus collective public sentiments are seldom expressed thereby.

Doubtless, elections are crude means of public communication with government. In simple-minded democratic theory they are represented as times when specific public preferences can be made known to government officials. More generally, they are occasions of "popular consultation" over policy matters (one of the components of democracy discussed in chap. 1 [Ranney and Kendall, 1956: 18–39]). But the defects of elections in this task are readily apparent. The voter's choice is typically between two candidates who discuss a variety of issues and policies but who do so with no specificity. Many issues are relevant to every election and may be of differing importance to individual voters and candidates. Candidate personalities and behavior affect voters, too, as does the record of the incumbent administration and, hence, its political party. How, then, can one read a specific policy message from the outcome of any election? And despite the faddishness of bemoaning the defects of contemporary campaigns and elections for such reasons, elections have always been limited in these ways as means of popular consultation.

There are several views of what elections might actually afford in the way of public influence over government (see chap. 3). But there is substantial evidence, too, that elections and parties are instruments for public influence of government, even if in more diffuse ways than simple-minded versions of democratic theory might suggest.

The Historical Tides of Electoral Participation

Mass participation is much like two-party competition: far more venerated in theory and in civics-text explications of U.S. government than its history would seem to justify. In colonial and postcolonial America participation was quite restricted by suffrage laws (chap. 2). Even the legally enfranchised were relatively "deferential" to the ruling leadership in the early years of the Republic and did not vigorously exercise the right to vote (Formisano, 1974). Generally democratic suffrage laws did not exist until the end of the Civil War—and those laws granted the franchise only to men. By the beginning of the twentieth century, of course, those laws had been undermined to disfranchise black males in the South. It was not until the 1980s that even polyarchic suffrage rights were widely, if not fully, assured in the United States. Through most of our history, then, only a minority of citizens were allowed to participate in elections.

Participation in elections is shaped also by the political and institutional context of the times. For example, in areas of extensive and meaningful competition among political parties, participation has been notably higher. Election and suffrage laws have also affected participation rates, in more ways than simply through the definition of voting rights. The dates and procedures for voter registration and for elections affect the participation of many citizens, and other requirements of election codes shape the competitiveness of the parties. Dramatic political controversies can stimulate turnout, as well, although their effects appear to be mediated by election laws and party competition.

The workings of these several institutional forces can be best illustrated by historical example. In terms of the rate of participation in elections by the legally eligible citizenry, the highest election turnout in our history was in the last third of the nineteenth century, during the Populist and Progressive eras. Several of the factors outlined here operated in that period to encourage participation. Dramatic and controversial policy issues divided the nation—beginning with the agrarian reaction in the 1870s to a variety of state and national economic policies and culminating in the 1890s in a debate over whether industrial or agricultural interests would be favored in national economic policies. A variety of new parties arose to compete for voter support over these issues, and the two major parties were forced to confront both the issues and the fledgling parties. Election laws afforded a means for parties to stimulate voter support directly. There were no secret ballots; voters used ballots given them by their parties. Further, registration systems were lax and could be manipulated by parties and political machines to ensure a high turnout of voters. Thus party leaders could easily encourage—even require—

voter support, and they could monitor the actual exercise of that support on election day by observing which party's ballot a given citizen cast into the ballot box.

But that combination of forces did not last very many years. Within that time the controversial national issues of the late 1800s were settled, and the major reasons for unusually high party competition were, hence, resolved. Party competition *within* the states also declined in the subsequent period, 1896–1932 (see chap. 3). The widespread adoption in the last third of the nineteenth century of the Australian, or secret, ballot—along with a variety of other "good government" safeguards against election manipulation—also weakened the parties' ability to deliver assured blocks of voters (Rusk, 1970). And in the South many potential voters were effectively disenfranchised by a variety of legal devices aimed at African Americans and lower-class whites (Key, 1949; Kousser, 1974). In sum, a combination of forces that encouraged high levels of voter participation gave way to one that discouraged participation. Not surprisingly, voter turnout in elections fell nationwide over the period 1896–1924.

Anticipated and Actual Voting Participation after World War II

At the end of World War II there still existed in the states electoral systems and contextual situations much like those that had been fashioned around the beginning of the century. In other words, one-party domination was still common in many states, and a variety of suffrage restrictions existed in a good number of them. Election laws that limited party manipulation of elections had been widely adopted, though they were not equally widely enforced, and the political issues of the time were not as divisive as those of the 1880s and 1890s. Thus one would have expected overall election participation to be lower than in the late 1800s. At the same time there was reason to expect considerable variation across the states. Some had two-party

75

competition. Some had no restrictions on the franchise. Some had a tradition of extensive public participation in politics, arising out of distinctive cultural norms about expected citizen responsibilities.

Based on the kinds of influences discussed so far, it was also reasonable to expect increasing participation nationwide in the period 1945 to the early 1990s. The elimination of most suffrage restrictions and the general loosening of barriers to voting should have stimulated both registration and voting. Increased two-party competition at the presidential level could have been fairly expected to increase competitiveness and turnout in other elections. The general advance of educational attainment in the population should have increased turnout, too. Studies of individual citizen participation have demonstrated a consistent and notable association between educational level and the propensity to vote: the higher a person's educational level, the greater the probability that he or she will vote in a given election. And after World War II the United States experienced a dramatic "educational democratization"—with remarkable percentages of young Americans completing high school and college. As the average level of education increased and as younger, better-educated cohorts of voters replaced aging, less well-educated ones, the level of participation would have been expected to rise, as well.

So much for theory. History has taken a different course. Nationwide, voter turnout indeed rose between the end of World War II and 1960. In the latter year turnout was 63 precent of the voting-age public, the highest level in the second half of the twentieth century. After 1960, however, turnout began to decline and continued to do so into the 1980s. Only slightly more than half the voting-age population has participated in presidential elections since 1980. And the trend of participation in state and local elections has followed that of presidential contests (Luttbeg, 1984; Karnig and Walter, 1989).

For its remarkable contradiction of what was plausibly expected, this decline in turnout has been labeled the "puzzle of participation" (Brody, 1978). That puzzle has preoccupied a number of scholars, but they have reached no consensus to explain it (see, for example, the competing views of Abrahamson and Aldrich, 1982; Cassel and Luskin, 1988; Piven and Cloward, 1988; Teixeira, 1987; and Wolfinger and Rosenstone, 1980). The turnout decline has particular relevance to this book for, as V. O. Key (1949: 508) has bluntly observed, "A government founded on democratic doctrines becomes some other sort of regime when large proportions of its citizens refrain from voting."

Despite all this attention, existing scholarship has not fully considered the implications that state-by-state variations in turnout have for democratic governance. Even superficial evidence indicates that such implications are a proper concern. Turnout has declined generally, but some states have remarkably higher levels of citizen participation than others. Still other states have dramatically higher levels of participation in the 1980s than they did in the 1940s. We must thus consider more than nationwide trends in voter turnout. Below those trends may exist distinctive patterns of state experience that have important implications for democratic theory. (For questions about how to empirically assess the level of voting turnout, see Appendix A).

Voting Participation in the 1940s

The democratic ideal envisions universal participation by the adult citizenry, but it also allows for some modest exclusions. Aliens, incarcerated felons, many of the mentally ill, and many convicted felons who have returned to society are typically disfranchised by state law. These exclusions appear justifiable and are doubtless widely approved. Voting by at least a good number of the rest of the "institutionalized population"—the aged, the chronically ill, or the handicapped—is impractical or physically impossible. After accounting for these and related minor exclusions, we should still expect at least 80 percent or more of voting-age citizens to vote regularly if a state is to qualify as *democratic*. Such turnout is commonly achieved in other Western democratic nations.

Turnout may fall below this level for many reasons, but my initial review of actual participation will ignore the causes of low turnout; if a state has low turnout, regardless of the reason, it is undemocratic. But I will later discuss some of the causes of the remarkably low participation in the various states.

I assess voting participation in the states in the period immediately following World War II by calculating the average percentage of citizens of voting age who voted in gubernatorial elections in each state in the period 1946–52.[1] *Democratic* states, again, exhibit participation by 80 percent or more of the voting-age population.

For a state to achieve a *polyarchic* rating on this trait, I expect participation to fall in the quite generous range of 51–79 percent of the voting-age public. Thus if a simple majority of voting-age eligibles actually votes, a state is accorded this rating.

With participation below half the voting-age population, a state must be judged *undemocratic*. When only a minority of citizens engages in this—the easiest and the most critical form of participation—there cannot be a democracy.

I judge states as *highly undemocratic* in terms of participation if turnout is one-third or less of the voting-age public. Clearly, only a narrow and select minority is engaged in the politics of such states.

There is one peculiarity about voting turnout in the 1940s that we must observe: in several of the one-party Democratic states of the South, voter turnout in primary elections was notably higher than in general elections. This was the case because only in the Democratic primary was there any real competition between candidates. In fact, Democratic party domination was so assured that the Republicans did not even run candidates for many offices. The general election was, then, only a formality to legitimate the outcome of the Democratic primary.

Students of southern politics conclude from this situation that the primaries were the "real" elections in this period (Ewing, 1949, 1953; Key, 1949). By this view we should use primary turnout as the measure of popular participation when it exceeded turnout in general elections. In certain respects I am uncomfortable with this view; the procedure would not fully indicate the extent to which general elections were a sham, and it would elevate the highly restricted degree of competitiveness in primaries to a level equivalent to that of elections in two-party states. V. O. Key himself was a harsh critic of one-party systems precisely because of the limited competitiveness even of their primaries. Nonetheless, primaries are doubtless a part of the overall election process, and participation in southern primaries in the 1940s was more meaningful for affecting election outcomes than was that in general elections. Thus I have based my judgments about the level of democratic participation on the higher of these two figures for elections in the 1940s. I believe that this procedure introduces a charitable bias into the evaluations of the southern states, but, as I will indicate shortly, that bias does not alter our ultimate conclusions about the extent to which voting participation in these states approximated democratic expectations.

With the preceding criteria we can consider actual turnout levels in the postwar period. Table 4.1 presents the relevant averages by state, with primary election turnout figures added when participation there was higher than in general elections. The average *nationwide* rate of participation in gubernational elections in this period was 51 percent of the voting-age public—at the bottom of the polyarchic range. As table 4.1 indicates, no state achieved a democratic level of turnout. Indeed, only five states had turnout of 70 percent or higher. Overall, twenty-seven states rated as polyarchies, fourteen as undemocratic, and seven as highly undemocratic. Perhaps most remarkable are the scores of the lowest-ranking states. Even having known generally what to expect from prior investigation of such data, I am still surprised at the participation rates in the lowest-ranking dozen or so

Table 4.1. Voter participation in gubernatorial elections, 1946–1952 (as percentages of voting-age citizens who voted)

State	Average Election Turnout (%)[a]		State	Average Election Turnout (%)[a]	
Alabama	22	(11)	Nebraska	56	
Arizona	44		Nevada	57	
Arkansas	25		New Hampshire	63	
California	49		New Jersey	50	
Colorado	59		New Mexico	51	
Connecticut	65		New York	54	
Delaware	73		North Carolina	42	
Florida	36	(34)	North Dakota	57	
Georgia	33	(13)	Ohio	58	
Idaho	57		Oklahoma	41	
Illinois	72		Oregon	49	
Indiana	71		Pennsylvania	50	
Iowa	56		Rhode Island	65	
Kansas	58		South Carolina	28	(3)
Kentucky	38		South Dakota	60	
Louisiana	46	(6)	Tennessee	34	
Maine	41		Texas	26	(20)
Maryland	39		Utah	70	
Massachusetts	67		Vermont	47	
Michigan	55		Virginia	17	
Minnesota	61		Washington	66	
Mississippi	33	(9)	West Virgnia	72	
Missouri	66		Wisconsin	59	
Montana	67		Wyoming	53	

(a) When average turnout was higher in primary elections, that number is listed first, followed by the average turnout in general elections (in parentheses).

Table 4.2. Voter participation in gubernatorial elections and
selected political characteristics, 1946–1952

Political Characteristic	Average Election Turnout (%)[a]	Number of States
Voting rights		
Highly undemocratic	32	12
Undemocratic	44	1
Modestly undemocratic	58	35
Party competition		
One-party	35	14
Modified one-party	53	21
Two-party	65	13
Election calendar		
Independent elections	35	5
On off-year U.S. congressional election ballots	43	8
Alternating between off-year and presidential ballots	53	27
On presidential ballots	63	8

(a) Percentage of voting-age citizens who voted.

states. Given the low participation, how could citizens at the time
even have imagined theirs were democratic states?

The rankings based on table 4.1 are not entirely surprising, of
course, because many of the states with low participation are those
that had highly circumscribed voting rights and one-party systems,
as indicated in earlier chapters. We can get a general appreciation of
the importance of the latter traits for participation, however, by way
of table 4.2, which presents mean turnout levels for states in each cat-

egory of voting rights and party competition identified in chapters 2 and 3. A similar breakdown is provided for another important institutional trait not so far discussed: the timing of state elections. We should not be surprised that turnout in state elections is especially high when they are held simultaneously with presidential contests, which stimulate exceptional voter interest. Similarly, we would expect that state elections held along with off-year U.S. congressional elections would have lower turnout than those in presidential election years and higher turnout than those held entirely independently. The scale for election calendars in table 4.2 reflects these expectations.

The results indicate how important voting restrictions were in reducing public participation and how much stimulus came from partisan competition and the nature of the election calendar. Participation rates were dramatically higher in states where voting rights were more democratic, party competition was greater, and state elections were held in conjunction with national ones. More specifically, states with especially restricted voting rights had only about one-half the turnout of those with the most generous voting rights. A similar range of variation is associated with differences in election calendars and party competition levels.

These findings reinforce an observation from chapter 2 about voting rights: two of the three insititutional traits considered here—the right to vote and the election calendar—were products of explicit political decisions and state laws. State law, in blunt words, directly circumscribed or enhanced the extent of democracy in both these ways.

The preceding results do not indicate the separate effects of the three institutional traits on voter participation. Some states in the 1940s demonstrated all the fortunate, or unfortunate, traits simultaneously. Illinois, for example, had relatively high voting rights and a two-party system, and it held its state elections along with presidential contests. Virginia, another example, had highly undemocratic voting rights and a one-party system, while holding its state elections entirely independently of national ones. Because a number of states demonstrated these reinforcing patterns of institutional traits, table 4.2 does not indicate the strictly independent influences of each trait on the participation level. Nonetheless, each is doubtless important for boosting or depressing public involvement in politics, and their interdependence does not affect the most important conclusions based on the data. No state achieved a democratic level of electoral participation in the immediate postwar period. About half were rated as polyarchies, partly because I adopted a very generous criterion for this rating. Had I required more than 60 percent participation, as an example, only thirteen states would have been included in the category of polyarchies. Twenty-one states were judged undemocratic in some degree and seven of these were, in fact, remarkably undemocratic.

Voting Participation in the 1980s

The analysis of contemporary voting participation used data for gubernatorial elections between 1980 and 1986.[2] In light of what is widely known about the decline in voting since 1960 most observers would not expect any of the states to rank especially high in the 1980s, even though turnout nationwide increased in the period between World War II and 1960. Going against the grain after 1960, turnout increased dramatically in selected states, especially those in the South, along with the expansion of suffrage rights. Thus nationwide voting trends since 1960 may not be a good guide either to the pattern in individual states or to the comparison of their 1940s and 1980s records.

Average nationwide voter turnout in gubernatorial elections between 1980 and 1986 was 46 percent of the voting-age public—a slight decline from the average level in the 1940s. That slip in the average conceals both laudable and unfortunate changes within individual states. A good number of states that had quite high turnout in the

1940s suffered a notable decline in participation by the 1980s, while several with poor records in the early period registered substantial increases (see table 4.3 for the individual state scores). In the 1980s, no state merited a democratic rating, and only sixteen rated as polyarchies, a sharp decline from the 1940s. The number of undemocratic states rose dramatically, to thirty, but only four remained in the highly undemocratic category. Once again, however, I must emphasize how charitable are these judgments. Had I adopted the criterion of more than 60 percent participation for a polyarchy, only three states would have qualified in the 1980s!

The three institutional political characteristics remained closely associated with turnout levels in the 1980s (table 4.4). There is less variation in turnout across the states in the 1980s than in the 1940s—fewer states having very low or very high scores—and this fact results in less dramatic differences across the categories of party competition, election calendars, and the right to vote. There are still, however, notable differences in turnout across the categories on each variable.

Turnout Levels and the Composition of the Electorate

Low voting turnout violates democratic expectations, and it has specific unfortunate consequences that are demonstrable. Low turnout indicates more than minority decision making. It also indicates that a *select* minority of citizens is determining election outcomes. This is the case for two related reasons. First, the likelihood that any American will vote in a given election is highly influenced by his or her education level, age, and income level. The higher one's education or income and the greater one's age, the greater the probability of voting. In other words, the higher one's social class, the greater the likelihood of participating in politics (Verba and Nie, 1987).

Equally important, the degree to which this class bias affects the composition of the actual voting electorate in a state is itself a product of the overall level of turnout. The latter relationship is common-

Table 4.3. Voter participation in gubernatorial elections, 1980–1986 (as percentage of voting-age citizens who voted)

State	Average Election Turnout (%)	State	Average Election Turnout (%)
Alabama	41	Montana	64
Alaska	55	Nebraska	48
Arizona	35	Nevada	37
Arkansas	48	New Hampshire	45
California	44	New Jersey	41
Colorado	43	New Mexico	41
Connecticut	45	New York	38
Delaware	53	North Carolina	46
Florida	37	North Dakota	65
Georgia	28	Ohio	41
Hawaii	46	Oklahoma	38
Idaho	53	Oregon	53
Illinois	42	Pennsylvania	39
Indiana	56	Rhode Island	53
Iowa	46	South Carolina	30
Kansas	45	South Dakota	57
Kentucky	38	Tennessee	35
Louisiana	50	Texas	30
Maine	52	Utah	63
Maryland	35	Vermont	53
Massachusetts	44	Virginia	33
Michigan	42	Washington	60
Minnesota	53	West Virginia	53
Mississippi	41	Wisconsin	44
Missouri	58	Wyoming	48

Table 4.4. Voter participation in gubernatorial elections and selected political characteristics, 1980–1986

Political Characteristic	Average Election Turnout (%)[a]	Number of States
Voting rights		
Modestly undemocratic	38	7
Polyarchic	47	42
Democratic	65	1
Party competition		
One-party	35	3
Modified one-party	45	31
Two-party	49	16
Election calendar		
Independent elections	41	4
On off-year U.S. congressional election ballots	43	32
Alternating between off-year and presidential ballots	50	4
On presidential ballots	56	10

(a) Percentage of voting-age citizens who voted.

sensical. When overall turnout is very high, it must be relatively high among all groups of prospective voters regardless of their social status. The reverse situation, very low overall turnout, need not logically show high disparities of participation based on social status, yet this is so in the United States because of the social class biases described above.

In general, then, the higher the voting turnout in a state, the more representative of the entire populace is the collection of voters. And

Table 4.5. Overall voting turnout and class disparities in voting in the states

Overall Turnout Rate in State, %[a]	Ratio of Lower-Class Turnout Rate to Upper-Class Turnout Rate (%)[b]	
	1982	1984
70 +	—	68
	(0)	(5)
60–69	71	64
	(8)	(28)
50–59	63	50
	(23)	(15)
Below 50		35
		(2)
40–49	55	
	(14)	
Below 40	49	
	(5)	

(a) Percentage of voting-age citizens who voted.
(b) Number of states in each category in parentheses.

the lower the turnout, the more unrepresentative are those who participate. Table 4.5 offers some evidence for this circumstance in two recent election years. To indicate the disparity in voting turnout by social class, the table compares the turnouts of low-status and high-status citizens in each state in the 1982 and 1984 general elections. High- and low-status individuals were indentified on the basis of educational levels, in keeping with the findings of Wolfinger and Rosenstone (1980) that education is the principal class-related attribute that influences the likelihood of voting. Lower-status individuals are those with only elementary school education, while high-status individuals have college degrees and postgraduate education.[3]

When the turnout of low-status citizens is equal to that of high-status voters, the ratio equals 100 percent. When the low-status turnout rate is half that of the high, the ratio equals 50 percent, and so on.

The results in the table confirm the expectation that higher overall turnout is associated with lower levels of class bias. And when overall turnout falls below 50 percent of the potential electorate—the cutoff point for achieving a polyarchic rating on the attribute of public participation—lower-class individuals are generally voting at half or less the frequency of high-status ones. In other words, a select subset of relatively high-status citizens is making election decisions for the entire state.

In the latter situation we would surely expect that the public policy decisions of government would be far different than those made in response to a democratically representative electorate. This expectation is itself supported by strong empirical evidence. Verba and Nie (1987: 267–85) have shown that high-status citizens have distinctive, and therefore unrepresentative, public policy preferences. Thus low voter turnout implies that unrepresentative and therefore undemocratic expressions of public preferences are being communicated to government in elections. Further, in collaboration with Jan Leighley, I have demonstrated elsewhere that an undemocratic state electorate of this kind is rewarded with state policies that favor its economic interests at the expense of those of poorer individuals (Hill and Leighley, 1992). When the poor are underrepresented in the voting electorate—in comparison to their representation in the general population—the state supports less generous welfare policies. The latter policies, of course, benefit the poor but are largely paid for by the middle and upper classes.

Conclusions

The evolution of voter participation in the second half of the twentieth century has been especially remarkable. A handful of states experienced dramatic increases, from embarrassingly low to modest levels of voter participation. A far larger number of states have suffered a sharp decline, from respectable, polyarchic levels of turnout to mediocre levels where less than half those eligible by age and citizenship are voting. The overall effect of these changes has been unfortunate, as well. In the 1940s twenty-one states, fewer than half the total, were judged undemocratic in some degree by my criteria for this component of democracy. In the 1980s, thirty-four of them, or fully two-thirds, deserved that label.

To make matters worse, there were good reasons to expect exactly the opposite development, as explained in my discussion of the "puzzle of participation." The causes of this decline are controversial, but their implications are clear. On this attribute politics in the fifty states has become considerably less democratic over the second half of this century.

5

Democracy in the States

We proudly call our government a democracy; yet ordinarily we have but a vague idea of what the word means.
William H. Riker

Political equality in voting rights, party competition, and mass participation constitute the three essential components of representative democracy. Each component must be satisfied in large measure if a government is, indeed, to be a democracy. Having evaluated the degree to which each of these three components was separately fulfilled in the states in the 1940s and the 1980s, I now investigate how they combine to indicate the overall pattern of democratization in each state. I can make more sophisticated judgments about the extent of democratization by taking account of combinations of states' scores on the component indicators, whereas prior chapters examined single indicators alone. Before proceeding with this investigation, however, let us recall our theoretical expectations about the complete requirements for democracy; we can then apply the empirical findings of the preceding three chapters to those expectations.

Political Systems in the States

If we take account of the different types of political systems that might exist in the states (chap. 1) as well as the components of democracy (chaps. 2–4), some of our theoretical expectations can be stated relatively precisely. In other words, we can now specify more systematic criteria for some of the possible regime types in the states.

For a state to qualify as a *democracy* it must rate very highly on all three of the component indicators: a state must exhibit fully guaranteed voting rights, two-party competition, and very high electoral participation by the voting-age population. The definition of "very high" public participation is likely to be arguable, but in conformity with chapter 4, I am designating 80 percent of the voting-age population as the lower threshold for the "very high" label. Some might think this standard a bit too low, too charitable, but regardless of whether we choose this or a higher standard for evaluating the individual fifty states, the conclusions we reach will be the same, as I will demonstrate.

The preceding definition of a democracy, which follows conventional scholarly wisdom, suggests how we might define some of the other possible regime types. Figure 5.1 shows the hypothetical possibilities in terms of the three specific component measures of democracy used in this study. We can imagine that those three measures define a cubic space that portrays the possible combinations of the three measures and, hence, the possible regime types. Individual states can be located in this space by their particular scores on the attributes of voting rights, competition, and participation. To qualify as *democratic,* for example, a state's component scores would have to place it in the upper right corner of the cube. That corner of the cube is where states with very high scores on all three component traits would be located.[1]

Other regime types, as identified in chapter 1, also fall within the definitional space portrayed in figure 5.1. To qualify as *highly polyarchic,* with a regime approaching but falling short of democracy, a state's scores would place it in the space approximate to, but just outside the "democratic" corner of figure 5.1, in the realm marked "HP." I can also translate the general definition of a polyarchy into

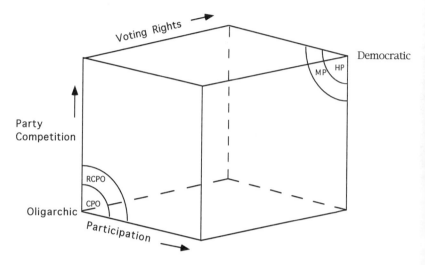

Figure 5.1. Political regime types.

a specific definition based on the three component indicators. To qualify as highly polyarchic, a state must first exhibit polyarchic voting rights as defined in chapter 2. That is, voting rights must be assured to virtually all adult citizens; only isolated instances of voting restriction can exist, although suffrage laws might still have some restrictive effects.

Second, a highly polyarchic state might exhibit a variety of combinations of partisan competition and participation; a relatively low record on one of these two attributes might be offset by a relatively high level on the other. In keeping with this idea, the "polyarchic region" in figure 5.1 can be conceived as somewhat curved, like a portion of a sphere that has been sliced so it has three flat surfaces, with the democratic region at its core. Some portions of this semispherical region will reflect relatively higher competition than participation, and some will reflect just the reverse. In more specific terms, I define this second requirement for qualifying as a highly polyarchic state as either (a) two-party competition and voter turnout in the range of 60–

80 percent of the voting-age public, or (b) modified one-party competition that leans toward two-partyism and voting turnout greater than 80 percent.[2]

Modestly polyarchic states are those that exhibit some relatively democratic characteristics but that still fall below the requirements for a high degree of polyarchy. The region of modest polyarchies is marked "MP" in figure 5.1. It is a still larger semispherical region with the highly polyarchic and democratic regions at its core. Under a more precise definition based on my component indicators, modestly polyarchic states must exhibit one fundamental characteristic and one of two possible combinations for the pattern of the other two characteristics. They might score as modestly undemocratic in voting rights, meaning that no identifiable ethnic or native group is regularly denied the right to vote, but such states might also exhibit malapportionment, gerrymandering, and generally restrictive suffrage laws. Before the reader reacts too negatively to this seemingly generous possible rating for voting rights, I emphasize that a relatively low score here must be offset by relatively higher ones on the other two component indicators. Thus a modest polyarchy must also exhibit, by my definition, either two-party competition and election turnout in the range of 51–60 percent of the voting-age public, or modified one-partyism leaning toward two-party competition and turnout between 60–80 percent. Even with somewhat restrictive voting rights, then, a majority or more of voting-age adults must participate in elections if a state is to qualify for this designation. And, in general, modestly polyarchic states are an identifiable group one degree further removed from the expectations of democracy.

At the other extreme of the range of possibilities, that is, for the most *undemocratic* of possibilities, we can identify two kinds of political systems. The most undemocratic possibility can be graphically identified as the corner of the cube in figure 5.1 labeled "Oligarchic," directly opposite the democratic corner. Recall from chapter 1 that an oligarchy is ruled by a select political elite, usually with a principal concern for its own interests. In terms of the three component variables used here, the oligarchic location in the figure indicates very restricted voting rights, a one-party system, and highly undemocratic voter turnout: one-third or less of the voting-age population. This combination of traits doubtless indicates a thoroughly undemocratic and highly oligarchic government. I call such regimes, falling near this corner, *closed party oligarchies,* or "CPO" in figure 5.1. These regimes are labeled *party* oligarchies because the single dominant political party is the organization employed by the ruling oligarchic elite, at least for appearances, to ensure control of government.

Additionally, we can conceive of governments that are highly oligarchic but that evidence somewhat more openness or participation and that, hence, occupy a semispherical region around the one for closed partisan oligarchies. This second category of undemocratic regimes I label *relatively closed party oligarchies,* the "RCPO" region in figure 5.1. In this category voting rights would also be very restricted, but the other two component variables might coexist in either of two ways. In some cases there would be modest party competition but very little participation, or, more precisely, modified one-party politics that leans toward two-partyism and voting turnout of less than a third of those eligible by age. In other cases there might be no competition but modest participation: a one-party system with voting participation in the range of 33–50 percent.

It is difficult to label any other regimes between the two extremes of democracy and oligarchy and between the particular regime types I have defined so far. Neither political theory nor common sense suggests a way to label those governments that have what we might crudely call "mediocre" overall scores in terms of the combination of traits that, at the extremes, would indicate either democracy or oligarchy.

Democratization in Individual States

Based on the preceding criteria and definitions of regime types we can rank the states from the most to the least democratic in the 1940s and the 1980s. The states that fall into the regime types defined previously can also be identified on the basis of those definitions and the scores on the three component indicators. To indicate the ranking of the states that fall in the middle, or "mediocre" range of regime types, we must rely on some additional procedures. I have used a multivariate statistical procedure to create an overall ranking of the democratization of the states, taking account of the combination of their scores on the three component indicators developed in the preceding chapters. In other words, for each of the two time periods under study I use states' scores on the ordinal scale for the extent to which the right to vote is guaranteed, on the interval-level party competition measure, and on the interval-level participation measure (the percentage of the citizen population voting in gubernatorial elections). Table 5.1 shows the result of that procedure: rankings of the states, from the most to the least democratic, and it ranks the states that fall into the five regime types identified previously.

The rankings are hardly impressive. In neither period does a single state qualify as democratic—in spite of the seeming generosity of some of my judgments about the qualifications for particular regime types. Only a small minority rates as polyarchic in either period and, to make matters worse, the number of polyarchies declines dramatically between the two periods under study. In the 1940s eleven states fall into the two oligarchic categories.

In the only positive aspect of the rankings, no states fall into either of the two extremely undemocratic categories in the 1980s. The "bottom" states are still a good deal less democratic than those with higher ratings, but at least they do not earn as unfortunate a label in the 1980s. There has been notable progress in some states, then, but the scores for the 1980s also indicate a broad movement toward "mediocre" performance in terms of expectations for democracy.

It is not surprising that the states with the poorest ratings in the 1940s are the southern ex-Confederate states. What may be surprising to many readers, however, is precisely how bad—how

95

Table 5.1. Democratization in the states

		1946–52	1980–86
Most democratic	Democracies:	—	—
	Highly polyarchic:		
		Utah	North Dakota
		Delaware	Montana
		Massachusetts	
		Washington	
		Illinois	
		Missouri	
		Indiana	
		Montana	
		Rhode Island	
		Connecticut	
		Minnesota	
	Modestly polyarchic:		
		Nevada	Washington
		West Virginia	Alaska
		Colorado	Delaware
		Nebraska	Maine
			Utah
Other states in order of decreasing democratization		Idaho	Nebraska
		Ohio	Iowa
		Michigan	Vermont
		New Hampshire	Missouri
		New York	Minnesota

Table 5.1 Continued

1946–52	1980–86
Wyoming	Oregon
Wisconsin	New Jersey
Pennsylvania	Indiana
Kansas	Illinois
South Dakota	Idaho
Iowa	Wyoming
New Jersey	Connecticut
California	New York
Maryland	South Dakota
Oregon	Ohio
North Dakota	Colorado
Oklahoma	California
Vermont	New Mexico
Maine	Pennsylvania
Arizona	Kansas
New Mexico	Rhode Island
	New Hampshire
	West Virginia
	Wisconsin
	Michigan
	Arizona
	Hawaii
	Tennessee
	Nevada
	Arkansas
	Oklahoma
	Florida
	Massachusetts
	Virginia
	Kentucky
	Maryland
	North Carolina
	Louisiana

Table 5.1. Continued

		1946–52	1980–86
			Alabama
			Texas
			Mississippi
			South Carolina
			Georgia
	Relatively closed party oligarchies:		
		North Carolina	—
		Tennessee	
		Louisiana	
		Florida	
Least democratic	Closed party oligarchies:		
		Mississippi	—
		Georgia	
		Arkansas	
		South Carolina	
		Texas	
		Virginia	
		Alabama	

undemocratic—those states were: their governments did not even vaguely approximate the standards for democracy. They might have had the appearance of democracy, with regular elections and two parties in name, but there was no substance under that facade. And with no credible evidence that government by the people was operative there, we must label these governments oligarchic.

The southern states have made dramatic and laudable progress, but they still rate at the bottom of the 1980s list, and the contrast between them and the highest-rated states is still dramatic. Most of the southern states are still largely one-party or they lean toward being so. And election turnout is but a third to a half that of the highest-rated states. Thus even though the South has made dramatic political progress, most states there still have an equally dramatic distance to go to approximate even a polyarchy.

The Practical Meaning of Different Levels of Democracy

The rankings of the states in table 5.1 may appear highly academic and abstract. The average reader may ask, "So what? What difference might my state's ranking make for politics here?" There are some practical and quite important consequences that should be discussed immediately (see chap. 6 for details). The everyday political life of states is affected by where they stand in the rankings in table 5.1. Consider, for example, the contrast between Montana and Georgia, states at the two extremes of the rankings in the 1980s. Montana has a polyarchic system of voting rights, voter turnout in elections is relatively high, and there is two-party competition. In Georgia voting rights are still not fully assured, turnout is quite low—less than half that in Montana—and the state's political life is still dominated by a one-party system.

Imagine, then, how different is the political climate experienced by citizens in these two states. Levels of public interest in politics, of social and peer pressure to participate in politics, of debate about political issues, and of citizen efficacy with respect to influencing government must be wholly different. In Montana the political climate surely stimulates public interest and concern with politics. It enhances democracy. Two-party competition, in particular, increases public interest in elections and government. High participation increases peer pressure and the general level of discussion and debate about politics. In Georgia the political climate—lacking all these attributes—doubtless depresses public concern about government and public participation.

Government officials would be affected differently, as well, by the political climates of these two states. Elected officials in low participation, one-party states have much more discretion in their policy choices. They need worry far less about how the voters or the members of the other party might react. In relatively more democratic states government officials must be far more sensitive to public sentiments. They must, in fact, be more responsive to public preferences.

Thus there is more to these rankings of democracy than mere academic counting of angels on pinheads. There are meaningful differences in political life that directly affect citizens and their role in state politics.

Summary Measures of Democratization

The rankings and categorizations in table 5.1 by themselves constitute significant results of this inquiry. They indicate how our state governments compare, in fact, with the requirements we casually allege they fulfill. But those rankings alone are not satisfactory for addressing all the questions we might pose about the causes and consequences of different levels of democracy in the states. We might ask, for example, whether it matters in any important way that some states are more democratic than others. Do they produce different government policies? Do they treat their citizens differently? Are their procedures for making policy different? To answer such questions, we need a more refined and exacting measure of the differences in degrees of democratization across the states.

The numeric scores of the states on the three component indicators developed in earlier chapters provide the necessary information to create a precise, summary measure of democratization that takes account of the combination of each state's scores on the three original indicators. I have created such a summary measure using the statistical technique factor analysis. Factor analysis offers a method by which we can investigate the three component variables—concrete, specific variables intended to measure the more abstract concept of democratization—and determine whether they are actually measuring a common trait, based on the patterns of scores on the three variables across the states. In simple terms, if individual states generally score high on all three variables, low on all three, or even "mediocre" on all three, that is evidence that the three variables *converge*. They are measuring the same general or "underlying" trait because they all three produce similar rankings of the states. Factor analysis informs us of the extent to which this is the case. For instances when the convergence is quite high, the technique also provides a method to create a new variable, in this case a summary measure of state democratization, based on the combination of scores on the component measures.[3]

A summary measure produced in this fashion has three important qualities. First, it has a high degree of convergent validity. A measure with high validity is one for which we have considerable confidence that it measures the intended trait—democratization in this case. Attempts to measure abstract concepts like this one often engender a good deal of controversy. Demonstrations of validity are crucial, therefore, to convince others of the soundness of our measurement. Convergent validation, specifically, is based on the ideas by which factor analysis was explained. When our component indicators, themselves based on theoretical rationales, converge as described above, we can have considerable confidence in the validity of the summary measure constructed from them.

Such a summary measure also has a high degree of reliability, or accuracy (Kerlinger, 1973: 442–55). Seldom is the convergence of component variables perfect. They should converge or "go together" to a high degree, but some divergence will exist in the patterns of high, low, and mediocre scores for some states. In constructing the summary measure, factor analytic procedures assume that the convergent portions of each component measure are the accurate ones and that the divergent portions are errors. Thus the summary measure is more reliable than any of the separate component variables, because, in the language of statistics, it is based on the common variance shared by the component variables, excluding the discrete or error variance in the component measures.

Finally, the summary measure is simply of great practical utility. With it we have a single, high-quality, interval-scale measure of overall democratization which we can use in statistical tests of the causes or consequences of that trait.

Based on these rationales I used factor analysis to investigate the degree of convergence of my specific component indicators of democracy in the 1940s and the 1980s. The results were highly satisfactory. The component variables were shown to have high convergent validity; thus it was possible to generate summary measures of overall democratization that have high validity and high reliability.[4]

Construct Validation of the Democratization Scales and the Correlates of Democracy

In the most elementary way of critiquing the validity of a measurement, we should look at the empirical relations among the component variables used to construct the summary scale. If we conclude that the validity of the summary measure is high, it is because we find strong evidence that the three component variables are all measuring some common underlying trait. That fact, plus the theoretical argument that the component indicators are appropriate ones for the underlying trait we have in mind, supports the conclusion that the underlying trait is in fact what we think it is. But we could be in error.

Perhaps all three component indicators are biased in the same fashion and they actually measure some other general trait, or they might simply mismeasure democracy in the same biased way. Perhaps they do not offer a complete measure of the general concept and, instead, encompass only a portion of its complete meaning.

A second, more far-reaching approach to validation can be employed to allay such doubts. That approach, known as *construct validation,* asks whether we can demonstrate that our summary measure supports research findings in conformance with theoretical expectations. In other words, valid measures of democratization should be correlated with measures of other relevant concepts in ways that political theory suggests they should. Thus construct validation is fundamentally tied to theory and, for that reason, it is considered the most important approach to validation in the social sciences (Carmines and Zeller, 1979: 22–27; Kerlinger, 1973: 461–69).

I can provide strong evidence for the construct validity of the democracy scales. To do so, I rely on Robert Dahl's summary of the principal findings of empirical research on the causes and correlates of the democratization of national governments in his book *Polyarchy* (1971). Naturally, some circumstances relevant to the democratization of nations—such as the effects of foreign control—are not strictly relevant to the fifty states. But many of Dahl's generalizations about the politics of nations have virtually identical theoretical applicability to the states. There is even a state-politics analog to the matter of foreign control, as I will explain below.

In particular, Dahl observes four conditions that prior research has demonstrated to enhance the prospects for democratization and that are relevant to the states: (1) a high level of socioeconomic development; (2) a low level of objective inequality of "important political resources" such as income, wealth, and status; (3) low subcultural pluralism—meaning a society that is highly homogeneous with respect to ethnicity, language, religion, and similar cultural traits; and (4) beliefs of political activists that are compatible with democracy. In general, then, my measures of democracy in the states should be positively correlated with measures of socioeconomic development and democratically oriented political beliefs, and they should be negatively correlated with measures of inequality of "important political resources" and of subcultural pluralism.

I suspect, however, that the preceding theoretical expectations must be qualified with respect to their temporal application to the fifty states. For three reasons I hypothesize that the correlations predicted above should be stronger in the 1940s than in the 1980s. The first reason arises from considering the ratings of the states in table 5.1. The table indicates that in the earlier period there were especially remarkable differences among the states in regime type—in degrees of progress toward democracy, that is; in the 1940s there were both polyarchic and oligarchic states. In the 1980s the states were distinguished by more modest degrees of democratization, even if only a few of them met the standards for polyarchy. Because state governments are more similar today, there is less possibility that we will discover strong relationships between regime type in the 1980s, as measured by the democracy scale and other traits.

Dahl gives us a second rationale for the preceding expectation by considering the likely similarities among the states in economic and social development rather than in political traits. Dahl observes that the evidence about national governments indicates there are two "thresholds" in the relationship of social and economic development to democratization: first, the prospects for democratization are poor below a certain low level of development. Once a nation progresses beyond that level, its prospects for democratization increase greatly. Beyond a certain high level of development, however, further social or economic advances do not increase the likelihood or degree of democratization (Dahl, 1971: 67-68). Similar relationships might exist among the states. And it could be the case that by the 1980s most states had passed the high threshold of development. If that were true, then the differences in development that remained would not be particularly correlated with the remaining differences in democratization.

Finally, we might also expect these different temporal patterns of relationships because of federal government influences on the states. It is here, as well, that we have an analog to the influence of foreign powers on the democratization of some independent nations (like the influence of the victorious Allied nations on Japan and Germany after World War II). In the 1940s United States political regimes were the product of relatively independent, "naturally" arising indigenous forces. To the extent that differing levels of economic development, inequality, cultural pluralism, and political beliefs cause different levels of democratization, the relations among these several variables in the 1940s should reflect the "natural" expectations of democratic theory.

By the 1980s, of course, the federal government had involved itself extensively in the determination of certain aspects of procedural democracy in the states (see chap. 2). Thus we should expect that "natural" causal forces might be only moderately correlated with democratization in the 1980s in comparison with the 1940s. In other words, even states with poor socioeconomic development, high inequality, high cultural pluralism, and relatively undemocratic belief systems might be far more democratic in the 1980s than those traits alone would lead us to expect—precisely because Uncle Sam makes them be more democratic. Thus the correlations of these other traits with democratization would be reduced from what would otherwise be their "natural" magnitude.

Table 5.2 provides empirical evidence relevant to these several expectations about construct validation. The table presents Pearsonian correlation coefficients among the democratization scales and conventional measures of state economic development, economic inequality, ethnic heterogeneity, and political attitudes relevant to democracy. Economic development is measured according to median family income from the 1950 and the 1980 U.S. census.[5] Economic

Table 5.2. The correlates of democratization

| Construct Validity Measure | Democratization | |
	1940s	1980s
Income inequality	−.81***	−.47***
Ethnic heterogeneity	−.77***	−.61***
Political culture	−.68***	−.70***
Economic development	.79***	.35**

**p < .01
***p < .001

inequality is measured by means of the Gini coefficient of inequality in family incomes, also derived from census data for 1950 and 1980.[6] Subcultural pluralism is assessed by a measure of ethnic heterogeneity taking account of the major ethnic groups identified in census data.[7] Political attitudes favorable to democracy are measured on a scale of political culture—attitudes about the role of government in society and about citizen obligations toward government. The latter scale was originated by Elazar (1984) and refined by Sharkansky (1969) from projections about the political attitudes of the ethnic and national groups that settled particular states. Higher scores on the latter scale indicate political attitudes less favorable to democracy, so we should expect a negative correlation between this scale and democratization.[8]

The bulk of the correlations in table 5.2 are precisely as hypothesized. All four social and economic variables are highly correlated in the appropriate direction with the democratization measure in the 1940s. In the 1980s all the correlations are still in the appropriate direction and are of notable magnitude. Yet, just as I hypothesized might be the case, the correlations for three of these variables are notably lower in the second period. Remarkably, however, the correlation with the political culture variable is as robust in the 1980s as in the earlier time.

In general, then, these results provide strong construct validation for the democratization scales based on expectations derived from traditional democratic theory. Further, the subsidiary hypotheses about the likely declining relevance of these social and economic attributes for levels of democratization are partially supported, but most of the attributes in the 1980s were still correlated with democratization levels at notable magnitudes. Federal government pressures and other developments may have weakened these influences on state political systems, but they have not eliminated them.

There is one final critical observation about the utility of these summary scales of democratization. Some readers may have been uncomfortable with my efforts earlier in this chapter to define regime types like democracies, polyarchies, and various forms of oligarchy and then cast particular states into those types. Doubtless, those definitions will be controversial. The summary scales of democratization, on the other hand, are not subject to the same criticism once we have documented their validity and reliability. We may not know that the states with the highest rankings on these scales are precisely democratic or polyarchic, but we know that they are, indeed, systematically more democratic than states with lower rankings. We can be very confident that these scales array the states across a dimension of greater to lesser degrees of democratization, even if we are unsure precisely where on that dimension they fall. Thus these summary scales are constructed appropriately for answering both theoretical and applied questions about the causes or consequences of differing degrees of democratization in the states. (For those interested in testing hypotheses about such relationships, appendix B lists the states' scores on my component and summary measures of democracy in both time periods covered by this study.)

Conclusion

I have measured and described the extent of representative democracy in the states, and I have assessed the progress toward enhanced democratization over the second half of the twentieth century. Perhaps what is most remarkable about the results is the contrast with casual scholarly and public assessments of government in the states. Contrary to widespread rhetoric and belief, the states are not even generally polyarchic today. If we apply a standard definition of democracy systematically—if we take a common definition of democracy seriously, that is—we find that the majority of states rate quite modestly. Admittedly, a number of states have made considerable recent progress, moving well beyond their formerly oligarchic regimes. But in quite a few others once-polyarchic regimes have degenerated into something less laudable. We have considerable distance yet to go, then, even to achieve polyarchy generally in the states, but much of the recent movement has been in the wrong direction.

6

Does Democracy Matter?

I go for all sharing the privileges of government who assist in bearing its burdens.

Abraham Lincoln

For many people democracy is an end in itself, sufficiently desirable that there need be no other reason to justify seeking one. In essence, a democracy is popular self-government, the real goal for those who believe democracy is an end in itself. In effect, a certain morally preferable method for deciding upon government policies is their goal, regardless of what policies the people ask the government to pursue. Self-government is preferred to rule by a dictator or oligarchy.

Self-government has been exalted as a morally preferable form of government for other reasons, as well. A variety of popular and scholarly writers argue that participation in government affairs is ennobling for all citizens. As Harry Emerson Fosdick has put it, democracy is based on the assumption that "there are extraordinary possibilities in ordinary people." Individuals as well as the collectivity of citizens might reap moral benefits from democracy. And the actual policies made by democratic methods might come to reflect this moral quality, too. The *promise* of democracy described in chapter 1 might be fulfilled. Many Americans doubtless share this faith.

A skeptic might ask, however, whether there are any other substantial consequences of democratization, particularly in terms of the fifty states. Were we comparing the former Soviet Union under communism or Fascist Germany under Adolf Hitler with the United States, for example, that skeptic might readily accept that government policies, as well as the methods by which those policies were created, would be fundamentally different. But the fifty states, our hypothetical skeptic might think, must be far more similar in their governmental policies, regardless of where they fall on the summary scales of democratization.

This view might seem quite reasonable to many Americans. Do not all the fifty states appear quite similar in their public policies? Do they not have quite similar legal responsibilities under law? And are they not pressed into notable conformity and similarity by a national government that has usurped many of their powers in the twentieth century and has forced many common policies upon them? Indeed, there are plausible reasons for questioning just how different might be the policies of state governments regardless of differences in the internal processes by which those policies are made (as ranked in chap. 5).

Yet many academicians and everyday observers of political life assert that democracy matters for public policy and that it does so as a general rule, not merely in specific places and comparisons. Thus there are many who would expect to find support for a positive view of democracy in the activities of state governments. In this chapter I answer the skeptics and offer evidence that democracy does have notable consequences for the policies of the fifty states. I must forewarn the lay reader, however, that developing this evidence will be a detailed and extended exercise. The question of how political process characteristics like democratization affect public policies has been intensively researched. Yet that research has produced nearly as much disagreement as consensus among scholars. To do justice to a number of different scholarly points of view, I will carefully develop a rationale for the policy consequences to be expected from democratization. Further, I will consider different avenues by which those consequences might arrive and then present some modestly complicated statistical analyses to document which of the latter avenues is, indeed, the most prominent.

Democracy and Public Policy

A considerable number of policy changes have been hypothesized to be consequences of democratization. Three prominent hypotheses appear particularly relevant to the fifty states. First, a number of scholars have argued that democratization will inevitably lead to an increased government commitment to welfare policies favoring the interests of the poor or lower classes. As common as this expectation has been, it has been subject to a variety of emphases. Robert Dahl offers one of the best general statements of the hypothesis in his book *Polyarchy* (1971: 20–23), which summarizes the findings of empirical research on the causes and consequences of democratization. Of equal note to the present study, V. O. Key's (1949: 307–10) discussion of party politics in the American South in the 1940s makes essentially the same claim about American state politics. A legion of scholarly analyses have been based upon some version of these two views, and many versions of this general expectation appear plausible. But they all adopt the same basic logic, starting with the observation that the poor and the lower classes are those most typically denied equal consideration by government in nondemocratic political systems. The process of democratization affords political legitimacy to these classes and, hence, to their interests. Thus we would expect democratic governments to be especially responsive to the interests of such people: states that are more democratic should have more generous welfare policies.

Dahl and Key are especially careful in specifying the likely character of this responsiveness, however. Dahl (1971: 20), for example, postulates that previously unrepresented interests would be better served after "the transformation of a regime from a hegemony into a more competitive regime or a competitive oligarchy into a polyarchy." Dahl specifically noted that modest differences in the level of democratization—as separated the fifty states at many times in our history—might not be associated with discernible policy differences. The same expectation is implicit in Key's formulation. His condemnation of the lack of accountability in one-party southern states, coupled with his recognition of the franchise restrictions that existed there, suggest that systems where the degree of democracy is dramatically higher—not just higher in modest degrees—would be more generous to the have-nots.

These observations amount to qualifications to the general proposition about welfare policies, and they suggest specific patterns that are likely to appear in public policy comparisons for the fifty states in the 1940s and the 1980s. Based on Dahl's construction of the importance of degrees of democratization, we should find a stronger relationship between levels of democratization and welfare policy in the 1940s than in the 1980s. Democracy should matter more for welfare policy in the 1940s, in other words, because there were substantial differences among the states in regime type in that period. There were both polyarchic and oligarchic states. In the 1980s the states were distinguished only by considerably more modest degrees of democratization; policy differences might still have arisen based on these regime differences, but we should expect them to be of lesser magnitude.

We might expect this temporal pattern to arise based on federal government influences on the states, as well. In the 1940s both state political systems and state public policies were relatively independently determined. That is, they were far less affected by federal government cooptation or financial assistance. Because both traits were more independently or more "naturally" determined, the relationship between the two might also have conformed more closely to expectations based on democratic theory. By the 1980s the federal government had involved itself rather extensively in the determination of certain aspects of both procedural democracy and policy in the states. Even when one examines what are, strictly speaking, indigenously determined policies—as will be the case here—the external federal influence might affect the expected relation between process and policy, most likely making it weaker than anticipated. Such might be the case for the welfare hypothesis, for example, because federal government requirements and financial assistance might make the welfare policies of the less democratic states far more generous than they would "naturally" be. Even indigenously determined welfare spending might be higher than expected because of secondary influences arising out of federal aid or pressure.

These observations about temporal patterns appear reasonable, but we must recognize, first, that they concern the strength of the expected relationship between democracy and policy, not the question of existence of any such relationship. Even in a co-optive federal system the character of state government may matter for policy. Whether enhanced procedural democracy is based on indigenous or external forces, it may lead to the same political activities and public policies. In addition, while the anticipated temporal patterns are based on notable theoretical and practical rationales, they are not inevitable. They are suggested, in effect, by a second hypothesis about the expected strength of the relationship between democracy and specific policies under particular conditions. That second hypothesis, too, must be subjected to empirical analysis.

One other point should be observed about the character of these hypotheses and the theoretical expectations behind them. Two different scholarly points of view exist with respect to *how* democracy might affect welfare policy, or any other policies for that matter. The first view is essentially that of Dahl and Key summarized above: a notable increase in democratization will lead inevitably to more generous welfare policies. An increase in democratization—in voting rights, participation, and competition—means that more of the poor in particular have the right to vote, more of them will vote, and one or more political parties will at least periodically vie for their support. Thus democracy itself is not hypothesized to *cause* more generous welfare policies in a direct manner. Instead, by this view it inevitably leads to a variety of political activities that otherwise would not exist and that make governments more responsive to certain policy preferences.

The second view of how democracy might affect policy is a more restrictive one. Several scholars, including Dye (1984), Godwin and Shepard (1976), and Jennings (1979), have argued that political institutions only *facilitate* certain policy outcomes; they do not ensure such results. These scholars argue that a state's welfare effort would not increase simply because it became more democratic. Instead, its welfare policies would be more generous only if it became more democratic and if at the same time its citizens generally desired more liberal policy and hence their preferences could be more faithfully translated into policy by means of more democratic processes; one political party made an explicit policy effort to appeal to lower-class citizens, who would themselves be better able to participate because of enhanced democratization; or the state was unusually wealthy and could support all public policies at a relatively generous level.

In sum, the first view is that enhanced democratization inevitably leads to a series of political behaviors that produce more generous welfare and the like. While I will at times use a short-hand term and call this a "direct" link to policy, it is not exactly that. Intermediate behaviors and actions are required, but their occurrence is thought by Dahl and Key to be automatic. The second, so-called facilitative view is that the latter intermediate behaviors are not inevitable, and only when certain explicit behaviors arise will democratization affect policy. There has been a remarkable amount of scholarly controversy about which of these two views of political process characteristics is most accurate, and for that reason I will provide statistical evidence with respect to both of them.

Closely related to the hypothesis about the likely relationship of democratization to welfare efforts (whether it be direct or facilitative) is a second one that democratic regimes will provide especially broad civil rights guarantees to their citizens. Indeed, this is a fundamental assumption of democratic theorists and democratic activists alike. A particular version of this hypothesis is implicit in Dahl's (1971: 23) argument that democratization enhances policy responsiveness to the "desires or interests of the groups, segments, or strata not hitherto represented." This expectation is a dominant theme, too, of Key's discussion of politics in the South. Once again, however, we must be conscious of the likely effects of significant differences—as opposed to modest differences—in levels of democratization for the realization of this hypothesis. Thus we should look for the same temporal patterns in this process-policy relationship as were hypothesized for welfare policy. And we should consider whether democratization ensures or only facilitates such policies.

Finally, a third prominent hypothesis arises from a variety of other sources. It has been widely hypothesized that democratization leads to a larger public sector, to "bigger government," that is. Mancur Olson (1982: 36-75) argues that once freedom of private organization is allowed in a polity, the number of special-interest groups that can make successful claims on government will grow secularly over time, and they will be one of several notable factors that increase the size of government. Olson (1982: 94-114) even employs the fifty states for an initial test of a number of related relationships derived from this hypothesis.

Theodore Lowi (1969: esp. 68-72) offers a related vision of this process in his explication of "interest group liberalism" as the prevailing U.S. political philosophy. He argues that the lowering of "constitutional barriers to democracy" in the 1960s encouraged a process already in motion to expand the public sector in response to a broad array of interest group demands. Thus democratization increases the number and variety of groups that can make legitimate claims on government and fuels the growth of government. This same vision is shared by Samuel Huntington (1975: esp. 65–74), who argues that one cause of the growth of modern U.S. government was the "internal democratic surge of the 1960s," which led to unprecedented demands for welfare spending. Beyond Olson, Lowi, and Huntington a host of other writers implicitly or explicitly accept this third hypothesis. Because of its popularity with conservative political thinkers unhappy about the growth of government and its consequences, one might fairly label this a view of alleged perverse consequences of democratization. At the same time, this hypothesis, like the two preceding it, has a commonsensical plausibility that would make it convincing to many people—even some who do not share the normative opinions about big government of Lowi, Huntington, and the like.

Measuring Welfare and Civil Rights
Policies and the Size of Government

To test these hypotheses about the policy consequences of democratization, we need appropriate measures of indigenous state policies relevant to each one. We need to determine whether, in fact, greater degrees of democratization are either associated directly with, or whether they simply facilitate, more liberal welfare and civil rights policies and a bigger government establishment. For the hypothesis about welfare policy I will use three measures of policy over which states have discretionary authority. One of these is an indicator of a state's budgetary commitment to welfare policy, and the other two are measures of the scope or content of welfare policy. The *Budgetary Spending Index* is the ratio of: (1) the percentage of total indigenous state and local government spending on welfare, to (2) the proportion of the state population that is in poverty. Thus the measure takes account of the level of budgetary commitment to welfare in light of the level of need for welfare. In a sense, then, it is the most encompassing possible measure of state commitment to welfare efforts. The construction of this measure in the 1940s, however, is hampered by the limited availability of combined state and local government expenditure data in the immediate post–World War II period. Thus I rely upon the two U.S. censuses that precede and follow this period—those taken in 1942 and 1957.[1]

There is some debate, however, about whether a gross budgetary commitment measure like the one above is entirely sufficient, or even entirely accurate, as an indicator of the level of welfare commitment. Russell Hanson (1983), in particular, argues that such expenditure measures do not always represent the actual content of public policy. In response to this concern I also use measures comparable to Hanson's suggested indicators of the scope of benefits provided and of the individual benefit level for what is perhaps the most controversial of welfare policies, Aid to Families with Dependent Children. These measures are (1) the *AFDC enrollment level,* the percentage of poor individuals in a state who are enrolled in AFDC, and (2) the *AFDC payment level,* the average monthly AFDC payment to a state's AFDC enrollees.[2] Thus I have measures of the actual character of welfare policy as well as of the gross state commitment to welfare.

In both periods I also employ two measures of state-controlled civil rights policy to test the second hypothesis. Once again, data are limited for the 1940s, but I employ the *McCrone-Cnudde Civil Rights Scale* (McCrone and Cnudde, 1968) of civil rights legislation in three policy areas and the *Lockard-Dye Civil Rights Scale* (Lockard, 1968; Dye, 1969) of legislation and enforcement mechanisms.[3] For the 1980s I developed two original measures of civil rights policy: a *fair housing scale* based on both legislation and enforcement activities, and a *fair employment scale,* also based on both legislation and enforcement.[4]

To test the third hypothesis I employ two conventional measures of the size of government: *state and local government employees per capita* and indigenously raised *state and local government general revenue per capita.*[5]

Table 6.1. Correlations between democratization and selected public policies

Policy Measures	Democratization	
	1940s	1980s
Welfare policies		
Budgetary Spending Index, 1942	.69***	
Budgetary Spending Index, 1957	.66***	
Budgetary Spending Index, 1980s		.26
Average AFDC payment	.67***	.58***
AFDC enrollment	.05	.12
Civil rights policies		
McCrone-Cnudde civil rights scale	.60***	—
Lockard-Dye civil rights scale	.70***	—
Fair housing scale	—	.38**
Fair employment scale	—	.60**
Size of government		
Government employment per capita	.41**	.37**
Government revenue per capita	.49**	.38**

** $p < .01$
*** $p < .001$

Democracy and Policy in the States:
An Initial Empirical Test

The general expectation underlying all the hypotheses discussed above is that the more democratic a government is, the more of certain kinds of policies it will support. My initial test of this expectation—and of the three specific hypotheses—examines the explicit, unqualified relationship. Table 6.1 presents correlations between the degree of democratization in each time period and the various policy measures in the 1940s and the 1980s. In general, the results for welfare and civil rights policies conform to the expectation that greater democratization ensures certain policy results. The correlations for these policies are very strong in the 1940s. Two of the three dimensions of welfare policy and both measures of civil rights policy are closely associated with the level of democratization. The higher the degree of democratization, in other words, the more generous the welfare and civil rights policies. In the 1980s the correlations are generally more moderate and more variable. However, two dimensions of policy—the generosity of AFDC benefits for individual welfare clients and fair employment policies—remain highly correlated with the level of democratization in the 1980s. Thus while democratization remains well associated with some of the policy dimensions, there is some decline in the general strength of the relationship, as I also anticipated.

The results for the hypothesis about the "perverse" effects of democratization, relating to the effect on size of government, are more difficult to judge. In both periods the correlations are more modest than for the other two policy areas, and there is very little decline in the size of the correlations during the period between the 1940s and the 1980s. While there is some support for the "perverse" hypothesis, it is far weaker than that for the other two policy areas or, for that matter, for the hypothesis that the salience of democratization for welfare and civil rights policy would decline over time.

As even the statistical novice is aware, we cannot treat the correlations in table 6.1 as indicating causal relationships. One reason is that the democracy-policy linkage may be more complex than is indicated by these results: it may be only a facilitative and not a direct link. In addition, other characteristics of states besides democratization also influence these various policies. If we fail to account for these other influences, we may overstate the possible importance of democratization. Previous research on state government policies has indicated several variables that are likely rival explanations for levels of welfare and civil rights policies and for the size of government. To take account of these alternative possible explanations for policy differences among the states, we must employ multivariate statistical analyses. I will present such analyses both for direct democratization-policy relationships and for the combination of direct and facilitative types.

Multivariate Tests of Direct Democracy-Policy Linkages

Considerable research has indicated, first, that socioeconomic characteristics of states affect various public policies, especially those based on levels of public expenditure. Wealthy states, for example, generally have more generous welfare policies and bigger governments than do poor states. Some research even suggests that wealth is more important than political process characteristics like democratization for determining such policies. Thus one important "control" variable should be the *wealth* of the state, which I will measure by the conventional indicator of median family income.[6]

A second socioeconomic indicator of importance is the level of *social mobilization* in the state. Social mobilization refers to the degree to which the population is geographically concentrated and, hence, the degree to which social, cultural, ethnic, professional, and other groups can easily form and work to influence government in their interest. States with greater social mobilization have better-organized groups of citizens pressuring government for enhanced policies in a host of areas. Thus more generous welfare and civil rights policies and even bigger government in general might result from such pressures. For this reason I include in my analysis a conventional measure of social mobilization: the percentage of a state's population living in metropolitan areas.[7]

Another critical control variable is public preference for policies. Ideally, democratic government ensures that public preferences are faithfully translated into government policies. The skeptic who wondered whether U.S. state governments could possibly differ in their policies might think that most of them would be generally responsive to public preferences for policy in about the same degree, regardless of how democratic they are. By this logic public preferences would be a more important influence on policies than would the indices of democratization. In those states with relatively liberal citizens, welfare and civil rights policies would be especially generous and the government itself would be generally large.

Fortunately, we can test the accuracy of the latter expectation because of the path-breaking work of Wright et al. (1987) and Erikson et al. (1989), who developed a valid and reliable measure of the extent to which state populations were liberal or conservative in their political preferences in a time period essentially equivalent to the 1980s. More generous welfare and civil rights policies and bigger government establishments can all be fairly labeled relatively liberal policies. Thus the measure of *public liberalism* is a prominent rival explanation for why states differ on these particular policies.

Finally, we should also take account of the influence of the U.S. federal government on state policies. The scope of federal subsidy of some policies and of federal pressures with respect to the adoption of many others may have been a significant influence on state actions— at least in the 1980s. And the three policy areas under study here are particularly good examples of this possibility. Welfare spending, first, is heavily subsidized, regulated, and even mandated at times by Uncle Sam, even though the states have substantial discretion over the specific policy measures I have developed. Thus spillover effects at the least—when federal subsidy of some programs may make it possible for states to increase the generosity of other programs that they otherwise would not raise—may be a substantial influence on even these discretionary policies. Much the same could be said for the size of state and local government. It, too, might be influenced by subsidy and spillover effects arising out of the host of federal aid programs available to the states.

Even civil rights policies, which are not so directly subsidized by federal monies, might be affected in the same way. All federal aid comes with conditions requiring greater civil rights guarantees in a number of state programs and policy areas than would typically otherwise be the case. Thus the wide scope of federal subsidy and of federal cooptation of state and local policy discretion in the 1980s might reduce the degree to which indigenous democratization might be important for welfare spending, civil rights policies, or the size of government. Federal pressures might, in effect, "nationalize" these policies, as many argue has been the case, making all states relatively similar regardless of their indigenous politics and political structures. Thus I will use measures of *federal subsidy* or *federal influence* relevant to each of the three policy areas as control measures.[8]

My initial test of the democratization-policy linkage, which also takes account of these other possible explanatory forces, is one for direct effects, following the arguments of Dahl and Key. The methodology for this test is multiple regression analysis whereby we consider the individual and collective potency of democratization and the various control variables for explaining differences in states' welfare generosity, civil rights guarantees, and size of government.[9] These analyses are possible only for the 1980s, I reiterate, because no measure of state opinion liberalism is available for the 1940s. But the test is an especially demanding one in the 1980s. The simple correlations between democracy and policy in table 6.1 are weaker in this period, making it more difficult, to begin with, for the relationships to survive the controls. And there are several good reasons to believe democratization might be less important in this period—again, because of such factors as increased federal government influence, the general increase in the similarity of political structures and policies across the states, and so on. Thus if democratization retains a potent relationship with any of the policy measures in these analyses, we have especially good evidence for its importance.

The results of these initial multiple regression analyses are reported in table 6.2. For those unfamiliar with such analyses, the "stan-

Table 6.2. Public policy regressions with democratization and selected control variables

Standardized Regression Coefficients

Policy Measure	Democratization	Wealth	Fed. Gov't. Subsidy or Influence	Social Mobilization	Public Opinion Liberalism	R^2
Welfare policy						
Budgetary Spending Index	.135	.196	−.090	.269	−.304*	.53
Average AFDC payment	.427***	.483**	.175	−.116	−.239	.59
AFDC enrollment	.027	.160	.099	.311*	−.481***	.54
Civil Rights						
Fair employment	.432**	.256	−.181	−.061	−.115	.53
Fair housing	.204	.120	−.115	−.018	−.391**	.39
Size of government						
Government employment	.058	.706***	.092	−.858***	.147	.58
Government revenues	.011	.870***	.179	−.354**	−.091	.47

* $p < .05$
** $p < .01$
*** $p < .001$

dardized regression coefficients" indicate the relative ability of the explanatory variables (democratization and the control variables, that is) to account for differences in states' public policies (with a separate regression calculated for each policy in the table). Larger regression coefficients indicate variables with greater independent explanatory power—after taking account, too, of the power of the other explanatory variables. Further, those coefficients marked with asterisks are ones for which we can have especially high statistical confidence that the relationship with a policy measure is accurately estimated by the regression.

The results for the welfare and civil rights policies bear separate consideration. For the two policy measures from these categories where the original correlation with democratization was especially strong—the generosity of welfare policy as measured by the AFDC benefit level and fair employment policy—democratization remains independently very influential after taking account of the various controls. Wealth is strongly related to one of the welfare policies, and public opinion liberalism is an important explanatory variable for several welfare and civil rights policies. Democratization, then, does not have a universally powerful relationship with all these measures of civil rights and welfare policy in the 1980s, but we have good theoretical reasons to expect that it might not. Yet the degree of democratization is closely and directly associated with some notable policies that favor those "not hitherto represented."

The hypothesis about the "perverse" effect of democracy on government size, however, loses all its support when we take account of the control variables. Wealth and social mobilization are the most prominent predictors of size of government variables. Finding that wealthier states have bigger government establishments is probably not surprising, but the negative relationship between degree of urbanization and government size may be remarkable to some readers. Yet it likely indicates an economy of scale effect: the more concentrated the population is in metropolitan areas, the smaller the need for *per capita* government spending and employment. Regardless of the explanation for the latter relationship, however, the principal conclusion of these latter two regressions is clear. Higher levels of democratization are not associated with larger state and local government establishments.[10]

Multivariate Tests of Direct and Facilitative Democracy-Policy Linkages

In this section I provide empirical evidence on both direct and facilitative relationships between democracy and policy. These tests allow us to assess both of the possible linkages and to compare the support for each one. To test for the srength of the direct relationship here, I can use the overall measure of democratization, just as I did in the preceding multiple regressions. The test of democratization as a facilitator of policy outcomes is a bit more complicated statistically, and it requires the creation of some new measures. That is, we must develop measures for the relevant facilitative relationships, which can then be added to the preceding regressions. The relationships that would lead to more liberal policies, recall, might be of three kinds: (1) a high level of democratization coupled with a liberal citizenry, (2) democratization coupled with an especially liberal political party, or (3) democratization coupled with high wealth.

The measures of these facilitative relationships are "interaction" variables, created by multiplying a state's democratization score by its score on a second variable that taps the second part of the joint relationship. For the first relationship—democratization and liberal citizens—the second variable is public liberalism. The result of this multiplication is a new variable that, in effect, distinguishes those states that are both relatively liberal and relatively democratic from those that are only liberal or only democratic, and from those states that are neither.

To create the second interaction measure I multiply the democratization variable by an index of the degree of liberalism of a state's citizens who identify with the Democratic party—which, even when not remarkably liberal, is always more liberal than the Republican party (Brown and Wright, 1990). Thus we isolate those states that are highly democratic and have an especially liberal Democratic party, those that have one but not both traits, and so on. The third interaction variable is the product of democratization multiplied by the wealth control variable.

Once we have created these interaction measures, a proper test of their potency and of the facilitation hypothesis requires that we add them to each of the multiple regressions in table 6.2 and compare the new R^2s (the total variance in the dependent variable explained by each regression) to those in the direct effects models of table 6.2. Both the absolute size of the increase in R^2 and the statistical significance of the increase should be considered (Gujarati, 1988: 223-26). Table 6.3 reports those figures for the various regressions.

In six of the seven regressions there is no support for the facilitation hypothesis because the three interaction variables add only very modest additional explanatory power. With fair employment policy, however, there is support for facilitation. The increase in explained variance, which is both notable in absolute size and statistically significant, means that a combination of democratization and one or more of the facilitation conditions helps explain the degree of generosity of this civil rights policy beyond what is possible by the "direct" effect of democratization and the control variables reported in table 6.2.

Yet the full results of the multiple regression for fair employment policy provide strong evidence for the "direct" effect of democratization, as well.[11] The results indicate that democratization, wealth, public liberalism, the interaction of democratization and wealth, and the interaction of democratization and public liberalism all have notable independent relationships with fair employment policy. Thus democratization affects this policy by both the direct and facilitative avenues.[12]

126

Table 6.3. Tests of the facilitative relationship of democracy with public policy

Policy Measure	R^2 with Direct Effects Variables	R^2 with Facilitative Effects Variables Added	Increase in R^2 and Statistical Significance
Welfare policy			
Budgetary Spending Index	.53	.54	.01; n.s.
Average AFDC payment	.59	.62	.03; n.s.
AFDC enrollment	.54	.58	.04; n.s.
Civil rights			
Fair employment	.53	.69	.16; $p < .01$
Fair housing	.39	.45	.06; n.s.
Size of government			
Government employment	.58	.61	.03; n.s.
Government revenues	.47	.50	.03; n.s.

Conclusions

Democracy matters for public policy in the fifty states, and it does so in ways consistent with empirical democratic theory. In the late 1940s, when there were dramatic differences in democratization across the states, levels of democracy were highly correlated with differences in both welfare and civil rights efforts, as predicted. My more detailed analyses for the 1980s also demonstrate notable support for direct linkages between democratization and some public policies—even after taking account of the influence of the most prominent alternative explanations. Further, democratization was linked in both direct and facilitative ways with one of the measures of civil rights policy in the 1980s, but my analyses provide more support for direct than for facilitative relationships.

In practical terms these findings mean, first, that the states that are more democratic adopt more equitable policies than do less democratic ones. That conclusion will be controversial among some of my readers, in part because I have not explicitly raised the idea of equity before this point. Nonetheless, I believe the conclusion justified by the welfare policy analyses in this chapter. Undemocratic regimes typically favor the interests of elites at the expense of the rest of the society, especially the lower classes. Democratization allows lower-class citizens to press legitimate new claims on government, and it encourages governmental responsiveness to those claims. More generous welfare expenditures are examples of the resultant policies. Thus democratic governments are relatively more equitable, if not fully equitable, in their policies than are less democratic ones.

The civil rights policy analyses suggest a second, and quite obvious, substantive conclusion. States that are more democratic ensure a greater range of individual civil rights—in keeping with both academic and popular conceptions of what democracy implies. Democracy has consequences for policy, then, in ways that concern more than just the abstract theoretician. Democracy makes a difference for practical, everyday interests of individual Americans.

Obviously, the analyses in this chapter do not illuminate all the specific intermediate processes by which these policy connections are established. While I have considered some of those intermediate processes by testing the facilitation hypotheses, a number of other scholars examining the separate components of procedural democracy are exploring other intermediate connections.[13] But the microscopic details of these processes are less important for my argument than is the big picture. Despite the simplicity of the present analyses, the findings are notable for their broad scope and for their confirmation that democracy indeed has consequential and predictable relations with government policy.

7

A Conclusion—and a Beginning

*It is for this that we love democracy: for the emphasis it puts on character;
for its tendency to exalt the purposes of the average man to some high level
of endeavor; for its just principles of common assent in matters in which all
are concerned; for its ideals of duty and its sense of brotherhood.*

Woodrow Wilson

At the end of the twentieth century we are seeing an extraordinary
tide of democratic sentiment around the world. In Eastern Europe,
the former Soviet Union, Latin America, Africa, and Asia new regimes and new mass movements pursuing this goal have arisen with
stunning rapidity. Some U.S. observers have seen in these developments a remarkable irony. Much of the rest of the world is clamoring
for democracy while many Americans apparently feel disillusioned
with, and almost indifferent to, their governments. Public cynicism
about many aspects of government is high. Public participation in
elections has declined to a mediocre level nationwide.

Are we no longer the democratic model for the rest of the world—
as has often been alleged in the past? Do we doubt our own rhetoric?
Is democracy in decline in the United States?

Scholars, social critics, and politicians have spent a good deal of
energy debating these questions and suggesting various diagnoses for

the condition of the body politic and prescriptions for curing its ailments. Many average citizens have doubtless voiced their opinions about these matters, too. It has not been my purpose to suggest cures for these ailments or to resolve all the major questions about democracy in the United States. I sought in this book to answer a few simple questions: How democratic in fact is state politics? Where and under what conditions has democracy thrived in the states? Does democracy matter in terms of what government does? With straightforward, factual answers to these questions I believe we have a firmer base on which to erect proposals to improve our governments; much of the criticism of those governments is based on casual or unsystematic assessments of how and how well they function.

This book indicates that one form of democracy can work in the United States. Fair approximations of representative democracy do, in fact, exist in some states. Doubtless, the governmental process could be improved even in the best of these polyarchic cases, but these states are models nonetheless of relative success. And democracy "does what it's supposed to." By definition, government routines in the more democratic states are based on a relatively high level of general public consent and participation, which is informed by a competitive partisan debate over what those routines should be. And the more democratic governments produce the specific policies that both activists and scholars anticipate. As Winston Churchill once observed, such governments may not be perfect, but they are better than the alternatives.

"So what?" the skeptic might ask. One answer is that the evidence should help restore our faith in U.S. democracy. It can work. It does work tolerably well in some places. Thus gloomy, broad-brush generalizations about the sad state of U.S. democracy are inaccurate. They are simpleminded and superficial, failing to recognize the places where this form of government thrives. If it can work reasonably well in North Dakota, why not in Texas, in Nevada, or in Massachusetts?

Indeed, why not in the national government? There is reason to believe that all our governments could approach at least polyarchy, if not complete democracy.

I emphasize the importance of faith in democracy. Woodrow Wilson's remarks at the beginning of this chapter might sound foolish to many readers. We laugh at such remarks because we're too cynical, too wise by experience, we believe, to think that government can really serve such ends. But democracy may be like religion: perhaps it can only succeed if there is sufficient public faith in its promised rewards. If we lack that faith, we quit caring about our government and about ourselves as a nation. We don't give a damn, in modern parlance. And we quit taking our share of the responsibility for the maintenance of democracy.

But if we have that faith, we must bear our portion of the responsibility for the working of the system, and we must share some of the blame when government does not live up to our expectations. Indeed, democracy is a partnership between citizen and government, a demanding partnership for all concerned—citizen, politician, and public official. Without faith, we fail to respond to the demands on us as citizens, and the quality of the democracy declines.

There is a citizens' agenda here, then. We must give a damn about our government. We must shoulder our responsibility for how well it works. In the admittedly simple conception of procedural democracy, that means we must participate actively in government, especially in elections. Greater public participation is not only an elemental component of democracy: high levels of participation ensure a climate that invigorates other aspects of the democratic process. Political party competition is imbued with far more policy relevance if the public is active. Government officials become more attentive to public desires. Even private interest groups, often alleged to subvert the public interest, will operate differently if they must be concerned for general public preferences. The engagement of citizens in the governing process can thus stimulate actions by candidates for office, elected officials, and political parties as well.

There is a scholarly agenda here, too. Why has democracy thrived in some parts of our nation but not others? What conditions favor this form of government? What impedes it? We may be able to use the answers to those questions for purposes of social engineering. We might, that is, use such knowledge to advance the spread of democracy throughout the nation.

An understanding of the roots of representative democracy would be useful, too, to those who desire more "advanced" forms of democratization. I argued in the beginning of this book that a careful assessment of the workings of representative democracy was an important, and neglected, beginning point for understanding our governments and their present performance. But such a system is the most elementary conception of democracy, even if it might be the only practical one for large modern societies. Many critics of our governments hope that richer, more thoroughgoing forms of democracy—with more extensive and more direct forms of citizen control of government—might be developed. Achieving a high level of representative democracy, or of polyarchy at least, may be a necessary first step in that process. If we understand the roots of this form of government, we may be able to fashion a climate for, and the mechanisms to support, the more advanced forms of this governmental system.

Measuring and Interpreting
Voter Turnout

Most contemporary analyses of voter participation assume that voting turnout levels are predominantly the product of individual citizen's motivations (see chap. 4). Most of this research is based upon opinion surveys of the general public, and it attempts to uncover relationships between attitudinal and demographic characteristics of individuals and their propensity to vote. Such studies include attitudes about government institutions, but the analyses rarely incorporate directly the institutional traits that might affect participation (for exceptions, see Patterson and Caldeira, 1983; Wolfinger and Rosenstone, 1980; and Piven and Cloward, 1988).

But we must recognize that voter participation levels are the product of a number of individual and institutional forces. Many voting-age Americans, as one example, have not voted at times because they were disfranchised by the laws and political practices discussed in chapter 2. Other characteristics of individual states such as the level of party competition also stimulate—or depress—citizen involvement in elections and, hence, affect turnout. Doubtless individual motivations—sometimes in response to partisan or government activities and sometimes entirely independent thereof—also affect participation.

When we consider the range of forces that influence voting, we should recognize that the standard ways of measuring and publicly discussing turnout are misleading for some purposes. Most government estimates of turnout—and, hence, most of those presented in the mass media—are calculated as the percentage either of the total voting-age population or of the number of registered voters who vote. The registered voter denominator is especially misleading for assessing aggregate turnout because there are many possible reasons for not being registered—ranging from indifference to the inability to meet restrictive registration requirements or to discriminatory enforcement of those requirements. Obviously, the relative influence of these different causes of nonregistration is important to evaluations of democracy, and using a turnout measure based on registration data would amount to ignoring the causes. There is good reason, however, to believe this denominator is problematic for any purpose, because estimates of the number of citizens registered are themselves of uncertain reliability (Piven and Cloward, 1988: 260–71).

Using the voting-age population as the denominator is also misleading for some purposes. In considering the turnout that is legally possible it produces an underestimate because some members of the voting-age population—aliens, those incarcerated in prisons, many of the mentally ill, many residents of nursing homes and other medical facilities, and convicted felons who have returned to society from prison—have customarily been disfranchised by law or practical circumstances. Thus the number of those legally allowed to vote is invariably smaller than the voting-age population, and estimates of voter participation will be higher when the number of those legally allowed to vote is employed in calculating turnout.

In addition, using the voting-age population yields a poor estimate of the long-term decline in legally possible voting turnout since World War II. As explained in chapter 2, especially large numbers of voting age citizens were disfranchised in the 1940s and 1950s by restrictive laws and discriminatory practices. Ethnic minorities were particularly affected, but many other Americans were also disfranchised by the restrictive registration laws, residence requirements for registration, and absentee voting rules of that period. Thus the legally eligible voter pool was especially restricted as a portion of the voting-age population. Over time, with the widespread loosening of suffrage laws, the legally eligible voter pool has risen to approximate more closely the voting-age population.

Figure A.1 offers a conservative estimate of the consequences of taking account of these observations. It presents two trend lines for voting turnout in presidential elections nearest the national census years from 1950 to 1990. These national elections were chosen because the coincident censuses provide data for some of the necessary calculations. Yet the conclusions from this analysis are equally relevant to state elections—for which appropriate data are not available for this demonstration. One series in the figure—labeled "VAP"—is the ratio of the total official presidential vote to the voting-age population. This series is the one most commonly used for estimating turnout in these elections (although varying estimates of the size of the denominator, even within the same government document, can produce slightly different turnout estimates for some of these years).

The second series—labeled "Adjusted"—first *adds* to the numerator of the VAP calculation two quantities: an estimate of the number of voters in some election contest on the relevant ballot but not in the presidential contest, and an estimate of individuals whose ballots were declared spoiled or invalid by election authorities.[1] Both these groups indeed participated in the relevant elections and should be counted as participants.

The second series is also derived by *deducting* from the original denominator—the voting-age population—estimates of the major groups clearly disfranchised by especially rigid registration laws, discriminatory legal practices, or societal pressure and discrimination. These groups include aliens, recent movers disfranchised by residency requirements for registration, institutionalized adults, members of

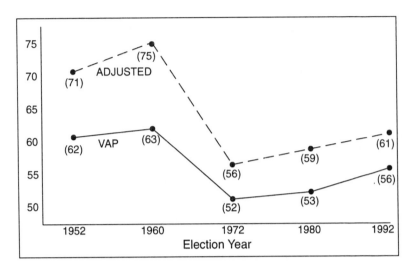

Figure A.1. Voter participation estimates for U.S. presidential elections.

the military disfranchised by residence and absentee voting requirements, and decreasing percentages of southern blacks.[2] The resulting
turnout estimates are conservative because numbers cannot be readily estimated for other groups who were also doubtless disfranchised.
They include some other ethnics, some southern whites who fell victim to registration laws aimed principally at blacks, illiterates in some
states in 1950 and 1960, and various other citizens across the nation
penalized by rigid suffrage requirements.

As expected, turnout is remarkably higher when calculated by the
adjusted method. In fact, even the higher figures underestimate the
differences in turnout that could theoretically be revealed between
these two methods. Because of the conservatism of the adjusted series, I suspect that at least 75 percent of those truly legally eligible
voted in 1952 and perhaps 65 percent did so in 1992.

These two methods of measuring turnout also yield quite different
estimates of the decline in voter participation in recent years. Voting
in presidential elections by those who were legally eligible—as mea-

sured by the Adjusted series—has declined by about 10 percentage points, or by 14 percent of its original level. The VAP series, which includes in its denominator many disfranchised individuals, indicates a turnout decline of only about 6 percentage points—equivalent to 10 percent of the 1952 level.

This simple demonstration should make clear that how we measure turnout is critical to inferences drawn from the data. The "correct" measure also depends on the question that is asked about election participation. My principal interest is how closely the level of participation approaches the democratic ideal. The preceding discussion suggests that the measure most faithful to that concern is the proportion of adult citizens who vote, with some allowance for those individuals in the institutionalized population, in particular, who are prevented from doing so. Voter turnout may fall below the universal participation of the full adult citizenry for a variety of reasons, but whatever the cause of such a shortfall, the implications for the *degree* of democracy will be the same. (Different causes of low turnout, of course, suggest problems of different degree and character.) The latter measure is the one, then, that was employed beginning in chapter 4.

The Individual Components and the Summary Measures of Democratization

In this appendix I provide the numeric values of each state's scores on the various measures used to assess levels of democratization. Thus I provide for each state, in both the 1946–52 and 1980–86 time periods, the scores for (1) the right-to-vote measure, (2) the degree of party competition, (3) the level of public participation in state elections, and (4) the summary indicator of overall democratization constructed via factor analysis from the preceding three component indicators. Table B.1 reports the values for the 1940s and table B.2 does so for the 1980s. The specific details by which these measures were developed are outlined in the corresponding chapters.

Table B.1. Values for the democratization variables for the period 1946–1952

State	Right to Vote	Party Competition	Public Participation	Overall Democratization
Alabama	1	3	22	− 1.881
Arizona	2	20	44	− 0.500
Arkansas	1	4	25	− 1.780

State	Right to Vote	Party Competition	Public Participation	Overall Democratization
California	3	23	49	.111
Colorado	3	39	59	.751
Connecticut	3	39	65	.903
Delaware	3	41	73	1.155
Florida	1	5	36	− 1.476
Georgia	1	0	33	− 1.673
Idaho	3	36	57	.628
Illinois	3	39	72	1.082
Indiana	3	37	71	1.008
Iowa	3	19	56	.193
Kansas	3	18	58	.220
Kentucky	3	25	38	− 0.121
Louisiana	1	0	46	− 1.342
Maine	3	16	41	− 0.261
Maryland	3	30	39	.025
Massachusetts	3	46	67	1.123
Michigan	3	36	55	.577
Minnesota	3	42	61	.874
Mississippi	1	0	33	− 1.673
Missouri	3	44	66	1.050
Montana	3	41	67	1.002
Nebraska	3	40	56	.689
Nevada	3	50	57	.965
New Hampshire	3	25	63	.515
New Jersey	3	25	50	.184
New Mexico	1	29	51	− 0.516
New York	3	34	54	.503
North Carolina	1	10	42	− 1.203
North Dakota	1	9	57	− 0.023
Ohio	3	34	58	.605

State	Right to Vote	Party Competition	Public Participation	Overall Democratization
Oklahoma	3	20	41	− 0.165
Oregon	3	19	49	.014
Pennsylvania	3	29	50	.281
Rhode Island	3	41	65	.952
South Carolina	1	0	28	− 1.800
South Dakota	3	15	60	.198
Tennessee	1	13	34	− 1.334
Texas	1	2	26	− 1.803
Utah	3	49	70	1.272
Vermont	3	12	47	− 0.205
Virginia	1	11	17	− 1.815
Washington	3	47	66	1.122
West Virginia	3	27	72	.793
Wisconsin	3	20	59	.293
Wyoming	3	34	53	.478

Table B.2. Values for the democratization variables for the period 1980-1986

State	Right to Vote	Party Competition	Public Participation	Overall Democratization
Alabama	3	17	41	− 1.830
Alaska	4	47	55	1.158
Arizona	4	35	35	− 0.206
Arkansas	4	17	48	− 0.340
California	4	35	44	.194
Colorado	4	37	43	.229
Connecticut	4	39	45	.397
Delaware	4	49	53	1.148
Florida	4	27	37	− 0.434
Georgia	3	14	28	− 2.527
Hawaii	4	21	46	− 0.271
Idaho	4	31	53	.436
Illinois	4	44	42	.461
Indiana	4	30	56	.530
Iowa	4	50	46	.876
Kansas	4	33	45	.159
Kentucky	4	17	38	− 0.785
Louisiana	3	17	50	− 1.430
Maine	4	39	52	.708
Maryland	4	10	35	− 1.195
Massachusetts	4	18	44	.479
Michigan	4	34	42	.066
Minnesota	4	36	53	.634
Mississippi	3	13	41	− 1.988
Missouri	4	33	58	.737
Montana	4	47	64	1.558
Nebraska	4	49	48	.926

State	Right to Vote	Party Competition	Public Participation	Overall Democratization
Nevada	4	30	37	− 0.315
New Hampshire	4	32	45	.120
New Jersey	4	47	41	.535
New Mexico	4	38	41	.179
New York	4	45	38	.323
North Carolina	3	23	46	− 1.370
North Dakota	5	38	65	2.425
Ohio	4	40	41	.258
Oklahoma	4	26	38	− 0.429
Oregon	4	35	53	.594
Pennsylvania	4	40	39	.170
Rhode Island	4	24	53	.159
South Carolina	3	19	30	− 2.240
South Dakota	4	23	57	.297
Tennessee	4	33	35	− 0.285
Texas	3	27	30	− 1.923
Utah	4	26	63	.682
Vermont	4	41	53	.832
Virginia	4	25	33	− 0.691
Washington	4	46	60	1.341
West Virginia	4	23	53	.119
Wisconsin	4	32	44	.075
Wyoming	4	36	48	.411

Notes

1. Is There Democracy in America?

1. Widespread efforts in the late twentieth century to achieve democratization in formerly nondemocratic nations have spawned new scholarly interest in how to define this form of government in a precise way. For some recent representative scholarly work that has explored the meaning and measurement of democracy, see Inkeles (1991).

2. Robert Dahl has employed the concept of polyarchy in a number of publications since the early 1950s. He has described such governments in somewhat variable terms and has, in particular, offered somewhat different lists of observable traits by which one might identify such governments (see, as examples, Dahl and Lindblom, 1953: 277–86; Dahl, 1971: 1–16; Dahl, 1989: 213–24). As is the case with many scholars' use of abstract social science concepts, however, there is a common conceptual meaning for the term throughout Dahl's writings (although I judge that meaning to be especially well expressed in his later works). It is this core conceptualization of polyarchy that I have adopted and explicated in this book.

3. For an introduction to the central theses of Marxism, and to the various strains of Marxist political thought, see Cox et al. (1985: 47–79).

2. The Right to Vote

1. These turnout estimates were calculated from population and popular vote data in the *Historical Statistics of the United States* (U.S. Department of Commerce, 1975).

147

2. Another legal requirement that significantly restricted voter registration and turnout in the 1940s was relatively long residency requirements for registration. For example, thirty-eight states required that a person live one or more years in the state before being eligible to register (Goldman, 1956).

3. Outside the South the voting rights of blacks were generally secure in the 1940s (Bunche, 1941). Blacks also voted in about the same proportion as whites in non-southern areas, as various case studies indicate (see, as examples, Collins, 1956; Glantz, 1959; Litchfield, 1941; McKenna, 1965; and Miller, 1948). Black politicians were well integrated in local politics in many cities, as well (Gosnell, 1935; Drake and Cayton, 1945; Osofsky, 1966). At the same time, however, even blacks outside the South suffered widespread discrimination in employment, housing, educational opportunities, and various public and private services. Myrdal (1944) discusses these problems and Weaver (1947) offers an especially useful survey of such discrimination in the North. The fact that blacks outside the South had the right to vote in the 1940s is important evidence that procedural democracy was ensured, but the *promise* of democracy, as discussed in chapter 1, was by no means equally affirmed in these states.

4. The best concise explanations of the Voting Rights Act, its extensions, and the political controversies associated with the law are provided in the appropriate annual editions of the *Congressional Quarterly Almanac* (1966 and subsequent years).

5. The eighteen-year-old vote was extended to all elections in the nation by the Twenty-sixth Amendment to the U.S. Constitution, adopted in 1971.

6. This provision was further strengthened by the Elderly and Handicapped Act of 1984, which required that voter registration sites and polling places in federal elections be made physically accessible to handicapped and elderly voters.

7. For a recent detailed account of how such practices evolved in a particular state, see Parker (1990), who chronicles the remarkable efforts to restrict the voting rights of blacks in Mississippi from the passage of the Voting Rights Act in 1965 into the late 1980s.

8. Voting rights activists also documented the relatively lax and permissive Voting Rights Act enforcement activities of the Department of Justice in the 1980s under the Reagan administration (see, for example, Days, 1984).

Thus the number of cases pursued by the department underestimates the frequency of actual violations.

9. Federal courts or the Department of Justice also voided or modified House of Representatives redistricting plans in Arizona, Illinois, and New York to eliminate minority vote dilution or to enhance minority political power. Courts also drew, or supervised the drawing of, redistricting plans in Arkansas, California, Colorado, Hawaii, Indiana, Kansas, Michigan, Minnesota, New Jersey, Ohio, and Washington because of other problems.

3. Political Party Competition

1. The Ranney index of state party competition is, for any given time period, the average of (1) the average percentage of the two-party popular vote won by Democratic candidates for the governorship, (2) the average percentage of seats in the state upper-chamber legislature held by the Democrats across all legislative sessions, (3) the average percentage of state lower-chamber seats held by the Democrats across all legislative sessions, and (4) the percentage of all terms of the governorship, upper chamber, and lower chamber in which Democrats had control. Unlike Ranney's presentation of the results of these calculations, however, I have rounded the final results to only two digits and then multiplied by 100 to produce a whole-number index.

Following Ranney, the index was based only on control of the governorship in Nebraska in both periods and in Minnesota in the 1940s because of the nonpartisan character of legislative elections. An examination of a variety of other election results in these two states suggested, however, that basing the index on the governor's race alone gave an accurate portrayal of general party competition.

The data sources for these calculations were principally: (1) for gubernatorial election results—Scammon (1956) and succeeding volumes; (2) for legislative election results in the 1940s—the *Book of the States, 1945-46* (1945) and succeeding volumes and their annual supplements; and (3) for legislative election results in the 1980s—the *Book of the States, 1988-89* (1988) and succeeding volumes, and the *Statistical Abstract of the United States, 1986* (1986) and succeeding volumes.

2. The data on party competition in presidential elections were taken from the *Statistical Abstract of the United States, 1950* (1950) and succeeding

volumes. In Alabama and Mississippi, votes for the indigenous States Rights Democratic party were used in the calculation of party competition in 1948 instead of those for the national Democratic party candidates.

3. Marxist scholars have been especially critical of the restrictiveness of election laws and their influence on minor party development (see, as an example, Parenti, 1988: 177–84). Admittedly, these scholars are concerned more with restrictions on progressive or avowedly socialist parties rather than on one or the other of the two mainstream parties. The Marxist view is that both major parties are essentially controlled by the dominant capitalist elite.

More generally, all parties are restricted in notable ways by state law (Lawson, 1987), but the weight of those restrictions surely falls less heavily on dominant parties.

4. Participation in Elections

1. This period was chosen to ensure that at least two gubernatorial elections were included in the calculations for each state. To achieve that goal for Virginia, however, I had to extend the time period to 1953. The estimates of the number of voting-age citizens in each election year in each state were calculated from U.S. Bureau of the Census data (1975: 1071–72, 1077–78). The total number of votes cast in each gubernatorial general election was derived from Scammon (1956). Voting turnout in primary elections was taken from the *Book of the States, 1952–53* (1952: 88); *Book of the States, 1954–55* (1954: 87); Heard and Strong (1970); and Ewing (1953).

2. The only available estimates of voting-age citizens by state in the 1980s—for the denominator in this calculation—are those for the 1980 census year. Thus I had to estimate that number for subsequent election years based on the proportion of aliens in the total population of a given state in 1980. Likewise, I employed data from 1980 on the ratio of the total voting-age population to the total population and used that ratio to arrive at an estimate of voting-age aliens based on the total number of aliens estimated for each state for each election year. In the vast majority of states, however, aliens are a quite small percentage of the total population. Thus the difficulties of this estimation process were considerably reduced. Finally, in the cases of Kentucky, Louisiana, and Mississippi 1979 election results were included so that at least two elections would be employed for every state.

3. The data for these calculations were taken from the U.S. Department of Commerce's *"Current Population Survey: Voter Supplement Files"* for 1982 and 1984, which are themselves data collections from national surveys of 71,000 households. Thus the subsamples of respondents for each state are large enough to generate reliable estimates of turnout by social class. The estimates of overall turnout levels in each state are also taken from the *"Current Population Survey."* The data were made available by the Interuniversity Consortium for Political and Social Research of the University of Michigan.

5. Democracy in the States

1. Political scientists have not reached agreement on how we might define as precisely as democracy the other possible regime types located in the cube portrayed in figure 5.1. Robert Dahl has suggested some nomenclature and implicit definitions for alternative regime types among nations in his book, *Polyarchy* (1971: 1–16), and I have adapted and expanded those ideas to fit the fifty states in my definitions of the regime types other than democracy. Doubtless, some readers might prefer different nomenclature for some of these types, but I suspect our eventual conclusions about democracy in the states would be quite similar regardless of the definitions of other regimes.

2. I have used the numerical criteria established by Tucker (1982) to determine the cut-points for one-party, modified one-party, and two-party systems on the Ranney scale. In addition, I have divided the numeric range for modified one-party states at its midpoint to determine which states might be labeled as leaning toward one-partyism and which toward two-partyism.

3. Factor analysis is a complex statistical technique that I have attempted to explain in simple terms for the lay reader. A more technical explanation of the technique for readers with at least moderate familiarity with correlational statistics is offered by Kim and Mueller (1978).

4. The factor analysis of the democracy component variables for the 1940s resulted in a single-factored solution with an eigenvalue of 2.51, which accounted for 84 percent of the variation in the three component variables. The 1980s factor solution also was single-factored, with an eigenvalue of 1.83 and with 61 percent of the component variation explained by the correlations

with the underlying factor. A variety of supplementary analyses of the component variables revealed no remarkable abnormalities in the relationships as to outliers, curvilinearity, and so on. Theta coefficients for the reliability of the composite summary measures created with the factor analysis were 0.90 for the 1940s measure and 0.68 for the 1980s (Carmines and Zeller, 1979: 60–62).

5. The median family income data are taken from U.S. Bureau of the Census (1952, 1983).

6. The data for the income inequality measures are taken from U.S. Bureau of the Census (1952, 1983).

7. The ethnic heterogeneity measure is based on the extent to which there is ethnic group diversity, employing data for the four ethnic categories non-Hispanic Anglo, African American, Spanish-surnamed, and "other races combined" (U.S. Census data for 1950 and 1980 and other U.S. government published data for the Spanish-surnamed population in 1950). The index is constructed using the formula for ethnolinguistic fractionalization in Russett (1964).

8. The Elazar-Sharkansky political culture scale is controversial because some researchers are split on whether it is a useful explanation of notable political attitudes, behaviors, or public policies. Yet it is the only measure available for all the states for the concept "political attitudes favorable to democracy." In my own research, further, I have found this measure useful for both descriptive and systematic empirical explanations of political phenomena (see, as examples, Hill and Hurley, 1988; Mladenka and Hill, 1989: 46–62). Any reader skeptical about the utility of this variable should keep in mind that it is only one of four being used for this multiple-measure, construct validity test.

States are arrayed on this measure from the most moralistic (with a scale score of zero) to the most traditionalistic (with a scale score of 9.0). Moralistic cultural values are precisely oriented to socialize individual citizens into a democratic, participatory ethic, while traditionalistic ones encourage conformance with an undemocratic system dominated by a semioligarchic elite. I assume that political activists, as well as the general public, share the dominant culture of their state, precisely as Elazar's conceptualization of each cultural type implies.

6. Does Democracy Matter?

1. In this and all other comparisons of public expenditure or revenue I employ state and local efforts combined. The reasons are, first, that states differ in the way they share policy responsibilities with local governments and, second, local governments are creatures of the larger state government and share in the form of government, be it democratic or otherwise, of the entire state. For the welfare budgetary commitment measure, further, the expenditure data for 1942 are calculated from the U.S. Bureau of the Census (1945: 37) and the U.S. Advisory Commission on Intergovernmental Relations (1967: 280). The 1957 data are calculated from U.S. Bureau of the Census (1974) and U.S. Advisory Commission on Intergovernmental Affairs (1967), while the data for my second time period are from U.S. Advisory Commission on Intergovernmental Affairs (1981). The estimates of the size of the population in poverty are from various years of the *Statistical Abstract of the United States*. For 1942, however, I used the percentage of each state's population that had no income—the only complete measure of a discrete low-income group available on a state-by-state basis from published reports on the 1940 census.

2. The data on average AFDC payments and numbers of families in the program in the 1940s are from "Current Operating Statistics" (1950: 28). The number of poor families is the number from the 1950 population census that had total incomes of $1,000 or less in 1949. For the 1980s I use federal government estimates of the number of people living in poverty, and the indices are derived from various years of the *Statistical Abstract of the United States* and from U.S. Social Security Administration (1980).

3. The temporal coverage of the McCrone-Cnudde Civil Rights Scale and the Lockard-Dye Scale extends only into the 1960s. I use them, however, because they are the suitable civil rights policy measures relatively close in time to the 1940s. Because of the more widespread adoption of civil rights policies in the states by the 1960s, using these two scales should slightly bias the results of my analyses toward finding a weaker relationship with democratization than if we used indices covering only the late 1940s and early 1950s. Knowing this fact in advance, however, we can take account of it in interpreting the results of the hypothesis tests.

4. The *fair housing scale* is measured on a five-point ordinal index that

distinguishes states having (1) no fair housing law, (2) a fair housing law but no enforcement agency, (3) a fair housing law and an enforcement agency judged by the U.S. Department of Housing and Urban Development as "not substantially equivalent" to the requirements of the U.S. Fair Housing Act, (4) laws and enforcement deemed "substantially equivalent" to the federal effort, and (5) laws and enforcement deemed to have far more extensive restrictions on allowable housing practices than the federal law. The information for this index is taken from U.S. Commission on Civil Rights (1985). The *fair employment scale* ranges from 0 to 10. States with no law receive no points. Two points are awarded those states having fair employment laws, an enforcement agency, and a record of sufficiently vigorous and effective enforcement to be designated a "certified 706 agency" by the U.S. Equal Employment Opportunity Commission—a status under which the EEOC defers to the state agency for initial processing of employment complaints. From one to five additional points are awarded depending on the extensiveness of the law's coverage: public employment, private employment, private firms according to number of employees, labor unions, apprenticeship programs, employment agencies, and state contractors. Finally, one to three more points are awarded depending on the extensiveness of statutorily defined limits on employment practices. The information for this second scale is taken from the Bureau of National Affairs (1989: secs. 401 and 405) and Larson and Larson (1988: sec. 9).

5. Both the state and local government employment and revenue data are from various years of the *Statistical Abstract of the United States*.

6. The distribution of states on the wealth measure is highly skewed and this variable thus violates the assumptions of correlation and regression analysis. For this reason I use the logarithm of the median family income in the succeeding statistical analyses.

7. The percentage of the population living in metropolitan areas is calculated from data in the *Statistical Abstract of the United States*.

8. For the welfare and civil rights policy regressions the "federal subsidy or influence" variable is defined as the percentage of total state and local government expenditures for welfare arising from federal aid; it is calculated from data in U.S. Bureau of the Census (1985). Even though civil rights policy is not literally subsidized by such aid, states are bound by a plethora of

federal civil rights regulations on the use of such aid, or any other federal aid for that matter. Thus the extent of federal subsidy is a fair indicator of federal influence over civil rights policies, too. For the size of government regressions, "federal subsidy" is defined as the percentage of total state and local government general revenue arising from federal aid; it is calculated from data in the *Statistical Abstract of the United States*.

9. All the regression analyses are based on forty-eight states, excluding Alaska and Hawaii because data are not available on those two states for the "Public Liberalism" variable.

10. Several recent studies have offered support for the argument that one component of procedural democracy, party competition, is less important for policy than is the presence of political parties that pursue different policies and, hence, offer policy-relevant choices to voters (Dye, 1984; Garand, 1985; Jennings, 1979). In light of these findings I tested the hypothesis that such parties or party systems might be more important in shaping policy than is the level of procedural democracy. To do so, I employed Dye's (1984) dichotomy of state party systems as "policy-relevant" and "not policy-relevant." I hypothesized that if policy-relevant parties were to have an effect on the level of welfare or civil rights efforts or on the size of government—the policy variables under study here—the reason would be an interactive relationship with the level of procedural democracy. Both policy-relevant parties and a political system open to those citizens who would generally press hardest for these policies, in other words, would be necessary to affect these policy measures. Tests of multiple regression models for both time periods yielded no instances when the appropriate interaction variable was found to be significantly related to a policy variable. In one instance, however, when the party system dichotomy was itself utilized as an independent variable, instead of the interaction term, it proved to be influential. The dummy variable had a simple correlation of $r = 0.52$ with the 1980s budgetary welfare expenditure index and was virtually as important as income in its contribution to the multiple regression equation. Because Dye's original formulation of this party dichotomy was based on welfare policy, we have evidence of the distinctive importance of party ideology when differences in procedural democracy across the states are modest. But because I achieved this positive finding in only one of a large number of tests with this variable, considerably more research may

155

be necessary to establish the interconnections among party, governmental structure, and policy.

11. These results are quite similar to those of Jackson (1992), who offers a number of tests of direct and facilitative relationships among several other political or institutional traits of states and their public policies. Jackson finds, as I do, stronger evidence for direct than for facilitative linkages.

12. Some readers might believe we should carry these analyses further and attempt to use a technique such as causal modeling to estimate the distinct influences of these several independent variables on public policy. There are good reasons, however, why this would be unwise. Causal modeling allows us only to estimate the importance of different independent variables based on the assumption that a specified causal ordering among the variables is the correct one. But Wright et al. (1987), building on a considerable body of earlier research, show that there is no scholarly consensus about either the causal ordering or the conceptual meaning of several of the socioeconomic and public preference variables used here—and in similar analyses. Thus we cannot theoretically justify any particular causal model upon which to base more sophisticated conclusions than those presented here.

13. For some recent representative work of this kind, see Dye (1984), Erikson et al. (1989), Hill and Leighley (1992), Jennings (1979), Nice (1983), Plotnick and Winters (1985; 1990), and Wright et al. (1987).

Appendix A. Measuring and Interpreting Voter Turnout

1. Based on the estimates of several observers summarized by Andrews (1966: 648-50) and on U.S. Bureau of the Census (1986: 9), I estimated the total participation rate to be 104 percent of the official, reported presidential vote in each election year.

2. Andrews (1966) offers an impressive but little appreciated estimate of "adjusted" participation for the 1960 presidential election. I followed several of his procedures for all the election years covered here and I used some of his estimates for 1960, but I did not exclude from the denominator all the groups that he excluded.

To calculate the effects of residence requirements, I relied on procedures and estimates in Yates (1962) and Andrews (1966) for the early elections, but also see Goldman (1956). For recent elections I used estimates in the U.S. Bureau of the Census (1976: 468) and Squire et al. (1987).

Blacks disfranchised in the South were estimated as (1) all those unregistered in 1952 and 1960, (2) half those unregistered in 1972, (3) and 10 percent of those unregistered in 1980 and 1992. The data on registration rates and numbers of voting-age blacks come from various editions of the *Statistical Abstract of the United States.* The estimates of the proportions disfranchised are based on the observation that many blacks were unconstitutionally prevented from registering to vote and others were dissuaded from voting, even if registered, because of discriminatory social pressures.

Numbers of aliens and institutionalized adults were taken from various editions of the *Statistical Abstract of the United States,* as were a variety of supplementary data for many of the calculations.

The estimate of adjusted turnout for 1992 is subject to more possible error than those for prior years, because some of the 1990 census and 1992 election data had not been released by the time I completed this book. Yet I believe any error in that estimate is only modest.

Bibliography

Abrahamson, Paul R., and John H. Aldrich. 1982. "The Decline of Electoral Participation in America." *American Political Science Review* 76 (September): 502-21.

Andrews, William G. 1966. "American Voting Participation." *Western Political Quarterly* 19 (Dec.): 639-52.

Banfield, Edward C., and James Q. Wilson. 1967. *City Politics.* Cambridge: Harvard University Press.

Barber, Benjamin R. 1984. *Strong Democracy.* Berkeley: University of California Press.

Beard, Charles A. 1914. *An Economic Interpretation of the Constitution of the United States.* New York: Macmillan.

Berelson, Bernard R., Paul F. Lazarsfeld, and William N. McPhee. 1954. *Voting.* Chicago: University of Chicago Press.

Blumstein, James F. 1983. "Defining and Proving Race Discrimination: Perspectives on the Purpose vs. Results Approach from the Voting Rights Act." *Virginia Law Review* 69 (May): 633-714.

Bollen, Kenneth A. 1991. "Political Democracy: Conceptual and Measurement Traps." In Alex Inkeles (ed.), *On Measuring Democracy,* 3-20. New Brunswick, N.J.: Transaction Books.

Book of the States, 1945-1946. 1945. Chicago: Council of State Governments.

Book of the States, 1952-53. 1952. Chicago: Council of State Governments.

Book of the States, 1954-55. 1954. Chicago: Council of State Governments.

Book of the States, 1988–89. 1988. Lexington, Ky.: Council of State Governments.

Bowles, Samuel, and Herbert Gintis. 1986. *Democracy and Capitalism.* New York: Basic Books.

Brody, Richard A. 1978. "The Puzzle of Political Participation in America." In Anthony King (ed.), *The New American Political System,* 287–324. Washington, D.C.: American Enterprise Institute for Public Policy Research.

Brown, Robert D., and Gerald C. Wright. 1990. "Ideology and State Party Coalitions." Paper delivered at the annual meeting of the American Political Science Association, San Francisco, Calif.

Bullock, Charles S., III. 1982. "The Inexact Science of Congressional Redistricting." *PS* 15 (Summer): 431–38.

Bunche, Ralph J. 1941. "The Negro in the Political Life of the United States." *Journal of Negro Education* 10 (July): 567–84.

Bureau of Indian Affairs. 1948. "Report of the Commissioner." In *Annual Report of the Secretary of the Interior, Fiscal Year Ended June 30, 1948,* 369–92. Washington, D.C.: U.S. Department of the Interior.

Bureau of National Affairs. 1989. *Fair Employment Practices Manual.* Vol. 8A. Washington, D.C.

Burnham, Walter Dean. 1981. "The System of 1896: An Analysis." In Paul Kleppner, Walter Dean Burnham, Ronald P. Formisano, Samuel P. Hays, Richard Jensen, and William G. Shade, *The Evolution of American Electoral Systems.* Westport, Conn.: Greenwood Press.

———. 1982. *The Current Crisis in American Politics.* Oxford: Oxford University Press.

Burnheim, John. 1985. *Is Democracy Possible?* Berkeley: University of California Press.

Carmines, Edward G., and Richard A. Zeller. 1979. *Reliability and Validity Assessment.* Beverly Hills, Calif.: Sage.

Cassel, Carol A., and Robert C. Luskin. 1988. "Simple Explanations of Turnout Decline." *American Political Science Review* 82 (Dec.): 1321–32.

Chambers, William Nesbet. 1963. *Political Parties in a New Nation: The American Experience, 1776–1809.* New York: Oxford University Press.

Collins, Ernest M. 1956. "Cincinnati Negroes and Presidential Politics." *Journal of Negro History* 41 (April): 131–37.

Committee on Appropriations, U.S. House of Representatives. 1987. *Departments of Commerce, Justice, and State, the Judiciary, and Related Agencies Appropriations for 1988, Hearings before a Subcommittee of the Committee on Appropriations.* Part 4: Department of Justice. Washington, D.C.: U.S. Government Printing Office.

Committee on the Judiciary, U.S. House of Representatives. 1982. *Extension of the Voting Rights Act, Hearings before the Subcommittee on Civil and Constitutional Rights.* Parts 1, 2, 3. Washington, D.C.: U.S. Government Printing Office.

Committee on the Judiciary, U.S. House of Representatives. 1985. *The Voting Rights Act: Runoff Primaries and Registration Barriers, Hearings before the Subcommittee on Civil and Constitutional Rights.* Washington, D.C.: U.S. Government Printing Office.

Congressional Districts in the 1980s. 1983. Washington, D.C.: Congressional Quarterly, Inc.

Congressional Quarterly Almanac, 1965. 1966. Washington, D.C.: Congressional Quarterly, Inc.

Cox, Andrew, Paul Furlong, and Edward Page. 1985. *Power in Capitalist Societies.* New York: St. Martin's.

Cronin, Thomas E. 1989. *Direct Democracy.* Cambridge: Harvard University Press.

"Current Operating Statistics." 1950. *Social Security Bulletin* 13 (March): 19–28.

Dahl, Robert A. 1971. *Polyarchy.* New Haven: Yale University Press.

———. 1989. *Democracy and Its Critics.* New Haven: Yale University Press.

Dahl, Robert A., and Charles E. Lindblom. 1953. *Politics, Economics, and Welfare.* New York: Harper & Brothers.

David, Paul T., and Ralph Eisenberg. 1961. *Devaluation of the Urban and Suburban Vote.* Vol. 1. Charlottesville, Va.: Bureau of Public Administration, University of Virginia.

Davidson, Chandler. 1984. *Minority Vote Dilution.* Washington, D.C.: Howard University Press.

———. 1992. "The Voting Rights Act: A Brief History." In Bernard Grofman and Chandler Davidson (eds.), *Controversies in Minority Voting,* 7–51. Washington, D.C.: The Brookings Institution.

Days, Drew S., III. 1984. "Racial Justice," In Norman Dorsen (ed.), *Our Endangered Rights,* 75–97. New York: Pantheon.

Derfner, Armand. 1973. "Racial Discrimination and the Right to Vote," *Vanderbilt Law Review* 26 (April): 523–84.

———. 1984. "Vote Dilution and the Voting Rights Act Amendments of 1982." In Chandler Davidson (ed.), *Minority Vote Dilution,* 167–80. Washington, D.C.: Howard University Press.

Dewey, John. 1937. "Democracy and Educational Administration." *School and Society* 45 (April 3): 457–62.

Downs, Anthony. 1957. *An Economic Theory of Democracy.* New York: Harper & Brothers.

Drake, St. Clair, and Horace R. Cayton. 1945. *Black Metropolis.* New York: Harcourt, Brace, and Co.

Dye, Thomas R. 1966. *Politics, Economics, and the Public.* Chicago: Rand McNally.

———. 1969. "Inequality and Civil-Rights Policy in the States." *Journal of Politics* 31 (Nov.): 1080–97.

———. 1984. "Party and Policy in the States." *Journal of Politics* 46 (Nov.): 1097–1116.

———. 1986. *Who's Running America?* 4th ed. Englewood Cliffs, N.J.: Prentice-Hall.

Elazar, Daniel J. 1984. *American Federalism.* 3rd ed. New York: Harper & Row.

Erikson, Robert S., Gerald C. Wright, Jr., and John P. McIver. 1989. "Political Parties, Public Opinion, and State Policy in the United States." *American Political Science Review* 83 (Sept.): 729–50.

Ewing, Cortez A. M. 1949. "Primaries as Real Elections." *Southwestern Social Science Quarterly* 29 (March): 293–98.

———. 1953. *Primary Elections in the South.* Norman: University of Oklahoma Press.

Fincher, E. B. 1974. *Spanish-Americans as a Political Factor in New Mexico, 1912–1950.* New York: Arno Press.

Fiorina, Morris. 1977. *Congress: Keystone of the Washington Establishment.* New Haven: Yale University Press.

————. 1981. *Retrospective Voting in American National Elections.* New Haven: Yale University Press.

Formisano, Ronald P. 1974. "Deferential-Participant Politics: The Early Republic's Political Culture, 1789–1840." *American Political Science Review* 48 (June): 473–87.

Garand, James C. 1985. "Partisan Change and Shifting Expenditure Priorities in the American States, 1945–1978." *American Politics Quarterly* 4 (Oct.): 355–91.

Glantz, Oscar. 1959. "Recent Negro Ballots in Philadelphia." *Journal of Negro Education* 28 (Fall): 430–38.

Glass, David, Peverill Squire, and Raymond Wolfinger. 1984. "Voter Turnout: An International Comparison." *Public Opinion* 6 (Dec./Jan.): 49–57.

Godwin, R. Kenneth, and W. Bruce Shepard. 1976. "Political Processes and Public Expenditures." *American Political Science Review* 70 (Dec.): 1127–35.

Goldman, Ralph M. 1956. "Move—Lose Your Vote." *National Civic Review* 45 (Jan.): 6–9, 46.

Gosnell, Harold F. 1935. *Negro Politicians.* Chicago: University of Chicago Press.

Gould, Carol C. 1988. *Rethinking Democracy.* Cambridge: Cambridge University Press.

Green, Philip. 1985. *Retrieving Democracy.* Totowa, N.J.: Rowman & Allanheld.

Grofman, Bernard, and Chandler Davidson. 1992. "Postscript: What Is the Best Way to a Color-Blind Society?" In Bernard Grofman and Chandler Davidson (eds.), *Controversies in Minority Voting,* 300–318. Washington, D.C.: The Brookings Institution.

Grofman, Bernard, Lisa Handley, and Richard G. Niemi. 1992. *Minority Representation and the Quest for Voting Equality.* Cambridge: Cambridge University Press.

Gujarati, Damodar N. 1988. *Basic Econometrics.* New York: McGraw-Hill.

Hanson, Russell L. 1983. "The 'Content' of Welfare Policy: The States and Aid to Families with Dependent Children." *Journal of Politics* 45 (Aug.): 771–88.

Heard, Alexander, and Donald S. Strong. 1970. *Southern Primaries and Elections: 1920–1949.* Freeport, N.Y.: Books for Libraries Press.

Hill, Kim Quaile, and Patricia A. Hurley. 1988. "Uniform State Law Adoptions in the American States: An Explanatory Analysis." *Publius* 18 (Winter): 117–26.

Hill, Kim Quaile, and Jan Leighley. 1992. "The Policy Consequences of Class Bias in American State Electorates." *American Journal of Political Science* 36 (May): 351–65.

Holmes, Jack E. 1967. *Politics in New Mexico.* Albuquerque: University of New Mexico Press.

Huntington, Samuel P. 1975. "The United States." In Michel Crozier, Samuel P. Huntington, and Joji Watanuki, *The Crisis of Democracy,* 59–118. New York: New York University Press.

———. 1991. *The Third Wave: Democratization in the Late Twentieth Century.* Norman: University of Oklahoma Press.

Hurley, Patricia A. 1989a. "Partisan Representation and the Failure of Realignment in the 1980s." *American Journal of Political Science* 33 (Feb.): 240–61.

———. 1989b. "Party Dealignment and Policy Representation in the House of Representatives: Comparing Opinion-Policy Congruence in the 1950s–1970s." *Congress & the Presidency* 16 (Spring): 37–55.

Inkeles, Alex. 1991. *On Measuring Democracy.* New Brunswick, N.J.: Transaction Books.

Jackman, Robert W. 1987. "Political Institutions and Voter Turnout in the Industrial Democracies." *American Political Science Review* 81 (June): 405–24.

Jackson, Robert A. 1992. "Effects of Public Opinion and Political System Characteristics on State Policy Outputs." *Publius* 22 (Fall): 31–46.

Jacobs, Paul W., and Timothy G. O'Rourke. 1986. "Racial Polarization in Vote Dilution Cases under Section 2 of the Voting Rights Act: The Impact of Thornburg v. Gingles." *Journal of Law & Politics* 3 (Fall): 295–354.

Bibliography

Jennings, Edward T., Jr. 1979. "Competition, Constituencies, and Welfare Policies in the American States." *American Political Science Review* 73 (June): 414–30.

Karnig, Albert K., and B. Oliver Walter. 1989. "Municipal Voter Turnout during the 1980s: Continued Decline." Paper delivered at the annual meeting of the Midwest Political Science Association, Chicago, April 13–15.

Keller, Suzanne. 1963. *Beyond the Ruling Class.* New York: Random House.

Kerlinger, Fred N. 1973. *Foundations of Behavioral Research.* New York: Holt, Rinehart, and Winston.

Key, V. O., Jr. 1949. *Southern Politics in State and Nation.* New York: Knopf.

———. 1956. *American State Politics: An Introduction.* New York: Knopf.

Kim, Jae-on, and Charles W. Mueller. 1978. *Introduction to Factor Analysis.* Beverly Hills, Calif.: Sage.

Knowlton, Clark S. 1962. "Patron-Peon Pattern among the Spanish Americans of New Mexico." *Social Forces* 41 (Oct.): 12–17.

Kousser, J. Morgan. 1974. *The Shaping of Southern Politics: Suffrage Restriction and the Establishment of the One Party South, 1880–1910.* New Haven: Yale University Press.

Ladd, Everett Carll, Jr. 1970. *American Political Parties: Social Change and Political Response.* New York: W. W. Norton.

Larson, Arthur, and Lex K. Larson. 1988. *Employment Discrimination.* Vol. 1. New York: Matthew Bender & Co.

Lawson, Kay. 1987. "How State Laws Undermine Parties." In A. James Reichley (ed.), *Elections American Style,* 240–60. Washington, D.C.: The Brookings Institution.

Litchfield, Edward H. 1941. "A Case Study of Negro Political Behavior in Detroit." *Public Opinion Quarterly* 5 (June): 267–74.

Lockard, Duane. 1968. *Toward Equal Opportunity.* New York: Macmillan.

Lowi, Theodore J. 1969. *The End of Liberalism.* New York: W. W. Norton.

———. 1975. "Party, Policy, and Constitution in America." In William Nisbet Chambers and Walter Dean Burnham (eds.), *The American Party Systems,* 238–77. 2nd ed. New York: Oxford University Press.

Luttbeg, Norman R. 1984. "Differential Voting Turnout Decline in the American States, 1960–1982." *Social Science Quarterly* 65 (March): 60–73.

165

Mayhew, David R. 1974. *Congress: The Electoral Connection.* New Haven: Yale University Press.

McClosky, Herbert, Paul J. Hoffman, and Rosemary O'Hara. 1960. "Issue Conflict and Consensus among Party Leaders and Followers." *American Political Science Review* 54 (June): 406-27.

McCool, Daniel. 1985. "Indian Voting." In Vine Deloria, Jr. (ed.), *American Indian Policy in the Twentieth Century,* 105-34. Norman: University of Oklahoma Press.

McCrone, Donald J., and Charles F. Cnudde. 1968. "On Measuring Public Policy." In Robert E. Crew (ed.), *State Politics,* 523-30. Belmont, Calif.: Wadsworth.

McGovney, Dudley O. 1949. *The American Suffrage Medley.* Chicago: University of Chicago Press.

McKenna, William J. 1965. "The Negro Vote in Philadelphia Elections." *Pennsylvania History* 32 (Oct.): 406-15.

Miller, J. Erroll. 1948. "The Negro in Present Day Politics with Special Reference to Philadelphia." *Journal of Negro History* 33 (July): 303-43.

Miller, Warren E. 1956. "One Party Politics and the Voter." *American Political Science Review* 50 (Sept.): 707-25.

Mills, C. Wright. 1956. *The Power Elite.* New York: Oxford University Press.

Mladenka, Kenneth R., and Kim Quaile Hill. 1989. *Texas Government: Politics and Economics.* 2nd ed. Pacific Grove, Calif.: Brooks/Cole Publishing Company.

Monroe, Alan D. 1979. "Consistency between Public Preferences and National Policy Decisions." *American Politics Quarterly* 7 (Jan.): 3-19.

———. 1983. "American Party Platforms and Public Opinion." *American Journal of Political Science* 77 (Feb.): 27-42.

Morehouse, Sarah McCally. 1981. *State Politics, Parties, and Policy.* New York: Holt, Rinehart and Winston.

Myrdal, Gunnar. 1944. *An American Dilemma: The Negro Problem and Modern Democracy.* New York: Harper & Brothers.

Naisbitt, John. 1982. *Megatrends.* New York: Warner Books.

Nice, David C. 1983. "Representation in the States: Policymaking and Ideology." *Social Science Quarterly* 64 (June): 404-11.

Ogg, Frederic A., and P. Orman Ray. 1942. *Introduction to American Government.* 7th ed. New York: D. Appleton-Century Co.

Olson, Mancur. 1982. *The Rise and Decline of Nations.* New Haven: Yale University Press.

O'Rourke, Timothy G. 1992. "The 1982 Amendments and the Voting Rights Paradox." In Bernard Grofman and Chandler Davidson (eds.), *Controversies in Minority Voting,* 85–116. Washington, D.C.: The Brookings Institution.

Osofsky, Gilbert. 1966. *Harlem.* New York: Harper & Row.

Page, Benjamin, and Robert Shapiro. 1983. "The Effect of Public Opinion on Policy." *American Political Science Review* 77 (March): 175–90.

Palmer, Monte, and William R. Thompson. 1978. *The Comparative Analysis of Politics.* Itasca, Ill.: Peacock.

Parenti, Michael. 1988. *Democracy for the Few.* 5th ed. New York: St. Martin's.

Parker, Frank R. 1990. *Black Votes Count.* Chapel Hill: University of North Carolina Press.

Patterson, Samuel C., and Gregory A. Caldeira. 1983. "Getting Out the Vote: Participation in Gubernatorial Elections." *American Political Science Review* 77 (Sept.): 675–89.

Piven, Frances Fox, and Richard Cloward. 1988. *Why Americans Don't Vote.* New York: Pantheon.

Plotnick, Robert D., and Richard F. Winters. 1985. "A Politico-Economic Theory of Income Distribution." *American Political Science Review* 79 (June): 458–73.

———. 1990. "Party, Political Liberalism, and Redistribution." *American Politics Quarterly* 18 (Oct.): 430–58.

Pomper, Gerald M., and Lederman, Susan S. 1980. *Elections in America: Control and Influence in Democratic Politics.* 2nd ed. New York: Longman.

Powell, G. Bingham, Jr. 1980. "Voting Turnout in Thirty Democracies: Partisan, Legal, and Socio-economic Influences." In Richard Rose (ed.), *Electoral Participation,* 5–34. Beverly Hills, Calif.: Sage.

———. 1986. "American Voting Turnout in Comparative Perspective." *American Political Science Review* 80 (March): 17–44.

Ranney, Austin. 1965. "Parties in State Politics." In Herbert Jacob and Kenneth N. Vines (eds.), *Politics in the American States,* 61–100. Boston: Little, Brown.

Ranney, Austin, and Willmoore Kendall. 1956. *Democracy and the American Party System.* New York: Harcourt, Brace and Company.

Riker, William H. 1965. *Democracy in the United States.* 2nd ed. New York: Macmillan.

Rusk, Jerrold G. 1970. "The Effect of the Australian Ballot Reform on Split Ticket Voting: 1876–1908." *American Political Science Review* 64 (Dec.): 1220–38.

Russett, Bruce M. 1964. *World Handbook of Political and Social Indicators.* New Haven: Yale University Press.

Scammon, Richard M. 1956. *America Votes.* New York: Macmillan.

Schattschneider, E. E. 1942. *Party Government.* New York: Rinehart & Company.

Schumpeter, Joseph A. 1942. *Capitalism, Socialism, and Democracy.* New York: Harper & Brothers.

Scott, Anne F., and Andrew M. Scott. 1975. *One Half the People: The Fight for Woman Suffrage.* Philadelphia: J. B. Lippincott.

Sharkansky, Ira. 1969. "The Utility of Elazar's Political Culture." *Polity* 2 (Fall): 66–83.

Simmons, Ozzie G. 1974. *Anglo Americans and Mexican Americans in South Texas.* New York: Arno Press.

Sly, John Fairfield. 1930. *Town Government in Massachusetts: 1620–1930.* Cambridge: Harvard University Press.

Squire, Peverill, Raymond E. Wolfinger, and David P. Glass. 1987. "Residential Mobility and Voter Turnout." *American Political Science Review* 81 (March): 1026–43.

Statistical Abstract of the United States, 1950. 1950. Washington: U.S. Bureau of the Census.

Statistical Abstract of the United States, 1986. 1987. Washington: U.S. Bureau of the Census.

Teixeira, Ruy A. 1987. *Why Americans Don't Vote.* Westport, Conn.: Greenwood Press.

Thernstrom, Abigail M. 1987. *Whose Votes Count?* Cambridge: Harvard University Press.

Tucker, Harvey. 1982. "Interparty Competition in the American States: One More Time." *American Politics Quarterly* 10 (Jan.): 93–116.

U.S. Advisory Commission on Intergovernmental Affairs. 1967. *Fiscal Balance in the American Federal System.* Vol. 1. Washington, D.C.

———. 1981. *Significant Features of Fiscal Federalism.* Washington, D.C.

U.S. Bureau of the Census. 1945. *Governmental Finances in the United States: 1942.* Washington, D.C.

———. 1952. *Census of Population: 1950, Characteristics of the Population.* Washington, D.C.

———. 1974. *Historical Statistics on Governmental Finances and Employment: 1972.* Washington, D.C.

———. 1975. *Historical Abstract of the United States.* Part 2. Washington, D.C.

———. 1976. *Statistical Abstract of the United States, 1976.* Washington, D.C.

———. 1983. *1980 Census of the Population, Characteristics of the Population: General Social and Economic Characteristics.* Washington, D.C.

———. 1985. *Governmental Finances in 1983–84.* Washington, D.C.

———. 1986. *Statistical Abstract of the United States, 1987.* Washington, D.C.

U.S. Commission on Civil Rights. 1959. *Report of the United States Commission on Civil Rights.* Washington, D.C.: U.S. Government Printing Office.

———. 1961. *Justice: Report of the Commission on Civil Rights.* Book 5. Washington, D.C.: U.S. Government Printing Office.

———. 1971. *Political Participation of Mexican Americans in California: Report of the California State Advisory Committee.* Washington, D.C.: U.S. Government Printing Office.

———. 1981. *The Voting Rights Act: Unfulfilled Goals.* Washington, D.C.

———. 1985. *Directory of State and Local Fair Housing Agencies.* Washington, D.C.

U.S. Department of Commerce. 1975. *Historical Statistics of the United States.* Washington, D.C.

U.S. Social Security Administration. 1980. *Research Tables Based on Characteristics of State Plans for Aid to Families with Dependent Children.* Washington, D.C.

Verba, Sidney, and Norman H. Nie. 1987. *Participation in America.* Chicago: University of Chicago Press.

Ware, Alan. 1987. *Citizens, Parties, and the State.* Princeton: Princeton University Press.

Weaver, Robert C. 1947. "Northern Ways." *Survey Graphic* 36 (Jan.): 43–47, 123–24.

Weeks, O. Douglas. 1930. "The Texas-Mexican and the Politics of South Texas." *American Political Science Review* 24 (Aug.): 606–27.

Wolfinger, Raymond E., and Steven J. Rosenstone. 1980. *Who Votes?* New Haven: Yale University Press.

Woodward, C. Vann. 1955. *The Strange Career of Jim Crow.* New York: Oxford University Press.

Wright, Gerald C., Jr., Robert S. Erikson, and John P. McIver. 1987. "Public Opinion and Policy Liberalism in the American States." *American Journal of Political Science* 31 (Nov.): 980–1001.

Yates, W. Ross. 1962. "The Functions of Residence Requirements for Voting." *Western Political Quarterly* 15 (Sept.): 469–88.

Index

Page numbers in italics refer to tables.

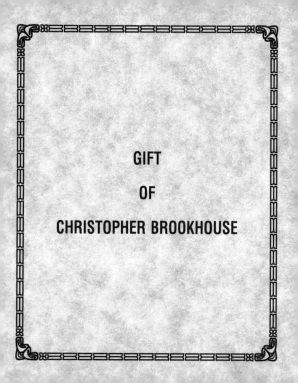

BLACK BOX

BY STEPHEN SANDY

POETRY

Black Box
The Thread: New and Selected Poems
Thanksgiving Over the Water
The Epoch
Man in the Open Air
Riding to Greylock
Roofs
Stresses in the Peaceable Kingdom

TRANSLATIONS

A Cloak for Hercules
(Seneca's *Hercules Oetaeus*)

Aeschylus, *Seven Against Thebes*

STEPHEN SANDY

BLACK BOX

P O E M S

LOUISIANA STATE UNIVERSITY PRESS

BATON ROUGE

1999

Copyright © 1979, 1983, 1988, 1990, 1992, 1993, 1994, 1995,
    1996, 1997, 1998, 1999 by Stephen Sandy
All rights reserved
Manufactured in the United States of America
First printing
08 07 06 05 04 03 02 01 00 99
5 4 3 2 1

Designer: Laura Roubique Gleason
Typeface: Janson Text with Copperplate display
Printer and binder: Edwards Brothers, Inc.

Library of Congress Cataloging-in-Publication Data
Sandy, Stephen.
    Black box : poems / Stephen Sandy.
        p.   cm.
    ISBN 0-8071-2368-4 (cloth : alk. paper). — ISBN 0-8071-2369-2
(paper : alk. paper)
    I. Title.
    PS3569.A52B58   1999
    811' .54–dc21
                                                98-51113
                                                CIP

For their encouragement, I would like to thank the editors of the following publica-
tions, where poems (sometimes in different form) were originally published: *Agni
Review, Antioch Review, aRude, Atlantic Monthly, Barrow Street, Denver Quarterly, Green
Mountains Review, Harvard Review, Hobart Park, Kenyon Review, Mudfish, Paris Review,
Partisan Review, Ploughshares, Salmagundi, Washington Square, Western Humanities
Review,* and *Yale Review.*
    "Great Plains Dooryard" appeared in the author's book *Man in the Open Air* (Alfred
A. Knopf, 1988). "Mammal Pavilion" appeared in another form in his book
Thanksgiving Over the Water (Alfred A. Knopf, 1992).
    I would also like to record my thanks to John Easterly, and to the Corporation of
Yaddo and the MacDowell Colony for their hospitality during residencies.

This publicaion is supported in part by a grant from the National Endowment for the
Arts.

For Allen Grossman

For Richard Howard

CONTENTS

ONE

DAPHNIS AND CHLOE

Looking at the grass for disease, thoroughly
unready. There was the sacral moment, the modern scare.
Natural enemies of the zebra mussel or the like. Slices or
slides of the engineered tomato. Playing the lottery here
with bovine spongiform encephalopathy

sailing along the sternocostal surface
sighting the great cardiac vein in blue the right
coronary artery in red. This is a mild
congregation I would say; now look out there
at the willow frond dribbling gold into the sun-breeze.

You have been here before, haven't you, we see only
moderately high snow drifts which may
be genetic, but still the most cynical regime
is prescribed. Some regression of course may be
possible but unlikely

so you may as well begin papering over
the walls that graphed the figure-ground relationship
in your life, or what you deemed it to be
while something else was happening, or it
was corruptly but minutely going by.

LATE CRETACEOUS REVERIE

We are never very far from
waking on the hillside of a past
we only imagined before, the whole
landscape of New Jersey down there in the gray of dawn
on the move; a slow restless milling,
parcels of green, a herd of Edmontosaurs,
lumbering sludge of life grazing.
And above it an official helicopter
hangs like a kite now the sun is up
laying its curved meniscus of roaring air
over the dazzled grasses, blush of sheen
like the green side of a hummingbird on the swale
where the hummocks of feeding backs
move not nor the long necks rise in wonder.
You lie back awake now considering
the relativism of this *fin de millénaire* day,
how few of the twinkling young consider breed
though celibacy is not yet an option
of their pairings. Down there
under a fern a dog gnaws at a white bone
big as a log.
The robin has returned to the
arborvitae beside the door
and has built its place of twigs and straw.
I will part the scented branches for a look
at the one egg there, the startling dark
turquoise, azure and sole as tropic noon
and wonder at the wetlands of the world
where from each plot of bog a whiff of mist rises
as dull footfalls continually plod.

PASTEL EVIDENCE

Such wranglers as you have never seen
hard yet credible from the mountains,
turning water off in the pass
at a spondee of steep buttes,
arranged a vale in the long Rockies
of leisure time, a place to pause
and hitch under the willow or
cottonwood by the stream where a man
in waders might spend hours with a fly rod
lightly scoring the sun-glossed currents
with fertile lashes.
                     Goodness,
there was much to detain us, the greenhorns—
a sod-roofed cabin limed with plaster
grouting, split logs bleached in the sun,
that history told us was the very spot
where Owen Wister made his home and quipped
"Pardner, when you say that, smile!"
—Don't let's miss Lord Selby on his paint
taking a morning canter before the dust
can rise from the dew on sagebrush trails
in this distant place, cooling his heels
while he rides out his mild but
unmentionable disgrace, our own
Sussex earl.
               Gramophone and flank
steak before the square dance; it must
have been Saturday night again! A nip
of bourbon behind the Indian blanket hung
at the window so others wouldn't see
us, sexual passion
crossing over like a bird of passage
far above the darkened cabin.

After the day's ride and currying down
our sweaty mounts, each one of us,
even wrangler Hank, bleached our hair
and polished boots; then the bird was sighted
wheeling over the valley, going to sulk
on some granite outcrop under the moon
watching the lights twinkle down valley,
our valley, dark and purple and still
as a Maxfield Parrish. O, too much
style; too little glory, too little
traffic. But it was beautiful, you said.

Yes, beautiful, but what are we
to make of that, because everything
that was crucial about it for us
got put away in the past, "put up"
as mother used to say of her plums
when July and boiling sugar made them
preserves, dark jars on a basement shelf?
Everything consequential about it
is unable to help, any more than a cat
can communicate in so many words.
Yet like a pet, what that *belle époque*
means is likely to be our feelings,
there on the table, not to be doubted.

                    Watersheds
brewed evidence, grumbling white
disclosures. Lord Selby went defunct
or had returned to Sussex, reconciled;
another guest would have spoken for his paint.
We wanted to read the final volume soon,
whenever it arrived at the trading post,
the whole three-decker then—our summer.
And grits with honey by the window edged
with flowering vines, strange trumpets
we would have called morning glories
back home, but these were so much bigger.

FINISHED COUNTRY

The bat stretches a puce wing
the forest lays down its arms
snow has mounted the hemlock bough
and a bouffant catafalque on April wires
your friends are facing the other way
the mountain's waist is zoned in mist

the orphan seizes the day
the sevens keep coming.
The snake's eyes peer
from under mossy eyebrows
where roots rock back on their heels
where chevrons of the blackbird signal.

Gears meshed: they took
Arthur and made him President
his peeling birthplace lingered upstate
the stream smoked from white tie and tails
lavender tongues of early bearded iris
ride the green spears, vulva, dolphins

the empty crater of a grapefruit half
shines on the trash heap, a reeking sun
and Lust goes about his weekly shopping
in splintered glasses: frolicking
mongrels at fresh scents pause with longing eyes
the ill-begotten tangle in wettest light.

OMELETTE PANACHE

It's so beautiful out here, she said;
blue sky and breeze on the hayfields—
I will forget about the people. He tried
to tell her the people would come
but she was happy without plumbing.

Why don't you stand up for what you believe in,
he said, instead of sitting there
like everyone else
or is that what you want,
to be seated without wiggling or getting up?

The urge to be criminal may be salutary,
she said; it's only a need for the toilet
too often denied, a kind of subaltern salvation,
to be redlined for disciplinary attention;
affection that is wholly impersonal

as Genêt in his hotel—and Christians about to lose
arms in the jaws of the Coliseum—discovered.
He gave in and said, let's play drop-the-soap
or Battleship. Then no one will switch
and we can meditate together.

All ready? On the count of three . . .
But she began to sob. He said,
no one will see you are pregnant if
you lean against the tree for a minute
and smile.

MY PLACE

—My loft, and how
you came

over letting your coat go
as if it was your room

already! And what I was
doing there is

not clear
to me—now—nor

why I am
standing here dumb

lips shaping amazing words
that fall forth duds.

Breathless, my pulse
is doing a waltz

through this room
and very same

"bachelor apartment" air
where, O, you were.

PRETZEL

Topiary before we got to Winding Hill
and other songs—Death Valley, Old
Depot, Bald Mountain, and the like.
Life is just full of coincidences
especially if you are wearing the right shoes
and get there on time without
too much confusion, timidity, or gnats.
At Mortar & Pestle Dry Cleaners we got

Tour de France dusters the owners never collected.
Looking for veronica and a whiff of elbow
you came laden with camera equipment
hanging out waiting for your scoop
going off with your smart apertures.
I flew onward alone, north
in my Mallard Sprinter, accompanied
by charm and ignorance and that old American

pie, this hankering for the open road.
When I got there the pretzels had been
picked over, though at the sidewalk sale
an occasional fuchsia love boat, or magenta,
showed up on the rack, if usually the wrong
size, not mine not yours. I bought a floppy
and headed for the Historic District.
At a basket barn I found an electric one;

handled the fuzz dreamily, fondled
the rust of my old life again and heard memory's
loose muffler barking hot ones
underneath. I loved you once, and for years, but now
the trees have stopped giving and the maple
syrup has been cut with corn. Can't do anything
about it because I don't even notice; can't
taste the difference, having forgotten you.

GREAT PLAINS DOORYARD

Here bricks are so rare they are like agates
we wonder who would carry them so far.
Here he feels good because he has nothing
he is thinking about
or that anyone would steal.
He has no status but this doesn't matter
it matters that no one can tell him why though.

When he walks home to the plain deal parlor
he is content that someone he loves
needs to be cared for nursed for a long time
and the bricks piled by the door are like cocoons
each one bends a little
arches ever so slightly.

She is already in the room and safe
though there was no buggy not even a horse.
It is a strange light she brings him
a kind of sodium splendor over the barnish dark.
All manner of thing will be well
but he must not care how it appears.

Once bricks were everywhere—
in the sky and underfoot.
That was grandfather's world
they were legion they were unnoticed.
Thinking about a brick was like trying to know death
but here they are so rare they are like agates
we wonder what carried them so far.

A STANDING EGG

The Vernal Equinox at last—
you'd have thought it spring half
balanced between the cold
and now burgeoning light
this sharpened drift reaching
into every moment and lifting

perfection out of it and
a little breath—now she said
on this day this day only
you can balance an egg on its
end with ease it will stay
like this will stand up like this

like lips parted ready to kiss.
One egg stood on the sill
for days then lonely firm
as a gymnast doing a hand-
stand on a ship's railing
at night—like the yellow jasper

head of an Egyptian
princess broken in half
by time, the plundering spade
of men. Now it is only
smooth chin and cheek a glossy
polish on jasper burnished

by light the curving surface
taut as an egg the lips
honey-golden, fragile
and lasting as human beauty
serious flesh that is opening
a relaxation outward

12

the full pause of the oval
mouth poised to suck in
the air of the aeons—O
parcel of human raised up for
the kiss of triumph of balance
the perfection the breakage of now.

GLOSSOLALIA

Listening to Chopin in Japan
a tongueless traveler observes
silences
       massive dance
of rush-hours on lumbering trains.

The Beatles hover on the air
as bells of a Moscow night on strange
winds across Siberia. He
walks in the valley of strange tongues
without a gift of tongues; may speak
when he may not be understood;
a music answers in him
something to which response completes
a common silence.
       Sibelius knew
grave subway builders going home
through warm November Tokyo alone,
made music of it; Bruckner wrote
       through the cold breakfasts and green tea
when sober women and their men
move toward work, as the hands of a fine
timepiece move toward the hour, silent,
careful not to spill a drop.

MAMMAL PAVILION

Three dolphins churn the un-Olympic pool—
too small, this watery socket—like a vase
with a bouquet of fins, white spray, black eyes.
High time: the trainer and her guards come on
laden with mikes; they put them to their tricks.
It is surprising, somehow, that they have names.

This one is Dixie, that one Rainbow, the third
is Mack. Terrifying volumes of our music
fill every aisle and wavelet; seem to rise
whenever their mistress bellows out commands—
or praise—to the dolphin trio. Rainbow is told
to let a member of the audience approach;
and kneel; and touch his crown, a tender place
and private, to judge from how the vigilant skin
winces and the shining body draws back toward
its element. It is a laying on of hands,
another way around; a blessing in reverse.
I see that places on a dolphin all
are private; sensitive, touching as dolphins do
no more than the old oceans streaming by;
flesh sensitive as ears, those dolphin ears—
how finely tuned!
                    The trainer shouts to us
over the echoes from applause. I watch them being
dolphins; make soggy tickets do for ear plugs;
and wipe the sea-spray from my face, enthralled.

                         *

The sea lion knows what he will do.
He'll do just what we tell him to.
He'll cruise, or limp, or hurtle through
his paces; will, if asked, halloo—
as if across some acreage of sea

bellowing his leonine degree.
Without a foot, he stands upon
his tiny stool, a paragon
of balance and mammalian grace!
A flipper-stand is commonplace,
although at clapping he's not apt.
In fact, the beast is handicapped.
When we consider all the tasks
he does when his stern master asks,
and watching the one long thew he is,
it's wonderful he's such a whizz.
The one reward that goes to him
is herring, at his trainer's whim,
but Pico does not give an inch.
He doesn't laugh or cry or flinch;
ignores the children in the bleachers,
the tourist's flash, the science teachers.
Alone in his midnight, marbly pelf
he dreams of a day he'll find himself
sniffing the breeze along the gleaming
foreshore of a rockbound bay,
hailing his lioness, the screaming
of the screaming children washed away.

*

The house lights dim. A screen rolls down to show
a film clip of the whales, slow blameless swimmers
cruising the booming shores of silence, through
endless hangars of salt cold, illumined
beneath the frosted pane of wimpling glass
the surface of the sea is when we view it
from below, the sky whales know before the other
sky. Calling and wailing, they keep their rounds,
fraught codes inaudible to human ears;
especially inaudible above
the sermonizing cello strains, a fulsome
sound track to impress us. As a final treat

we overhear the whales, those bloky Nereids,
singing each to each—vacationing
technologists have caught their eclogues on
a disc, like the passionate machinist who
collects axe-heads, arrowheads, celts. Always
the whales are passing into deeps off camera,
recede down rearranging halls of ocean.
Darkly they turn from us; resist their doom.

THESE VINEYARDS, THESE FARMS

O to be a shallot farmer, to have that self
respect; security of a crop everyone needs,
one you alone in your county can provide!

It sounds good, doesn't it? But instead
the valley is full of designer farmers, who count
on mega operations getting bigger

and suddenly it's like California
—or a soap of California. Acres to cherry,
miles of vines, miserable confections!

Then the politics of family agri-romance
become—or we discover that they were
to start with—a story by which we live

along the chainlink fences of a thruway.
Don't get me wrong! The Eddie Bauer is
a comfortable car, four-wheel drive and five

rear vision mirrors—a company car, one
of the few windfalls you find turning your place
into a corporation. It's a little

much. Notice, a minute after you start up
and get settled, it automatically locks, the new
high tech that wants to hold us; keep us safe.

FAR BE IT FROM ME

Turning around, turning, she wonders
what's in a name
this prodigious business of the leaves
whether hosta or funkia
she went out on a limb and marched forward

it is hard to see in cold weather you see
there a squint toward the sky a blinding light
as of lightning directly above
momentary blindness
she bought leeks mushrooms balsamic vinegar

but forgot the main course
do they ever serve nine-course dinners she wondered
what does that what could it possibly
mean to have *nine* she forgot
to buy what she needed

choosing vegetables was hard work
like picking a son-in-law
gently but firmly
grasp the body twist till it comes
don't worry about prickers

they'll come out with Lava soap
some fruits of the earth, melon, cucumber
aubergine snap off easily as beans
no twisting, for fear of bruising
better to snap fruit from vine

now where was—? let's see
if she knew who was coming for dinner
it is a commercial district and
everyone smokes and wears suits
it would be nice but

it is not like home not like the old days
when she knew just what it was
a name held in its wicker crib of consonants
for now it's now
and plenty of tenderloin.

THE AWKWARD AGE

Under the Twister Mountains, you know them,
down there in Liberty the girl with the won't-quit smile
was doing housework for her siblings, besides the
teaching. She had purpose on the brain. She stood
before all that energy and taught them day after day
American history. It was a joy but tiring;
yet the spirit of community service was on her.

Koreans were so much easier so, well,
keen. They didn't seem to mind
American history. She felt they were
happy to learn *aught* and it would come in handy.
They knew where they were going
because they were more or less there
lounging on the hustings of futures which

were pretty much decided for each;
doing a little hope but nothing harmful.
She remembered the Korean children,
they didn't have cash for shenanigans,
they smiled and got down to it
and tied their lunch satchels. Soon
they would be there. She saw Kip

standing for hours in front of his work. She
knew his work was what selected him,
what got him there. His work
advanced and showed great wallops of sight.
She guessed it was about bipolar feelings; he
had archery on the brain. It was
beautiful, finished, clean; on the button.

In the glissandos of coffee break
a shower of gratitude came down
as if the fume of poppies had kicked in;

her mind bounced like popcorn in the maker.
Poor thing, well meaning but
O so full of laughter, when no one,
especially she, knew what was up.

GOING FOR A SONG

As usual the son of good-name mid-class
city people spends his summer
with his parents
at his aunt's country house. If the guest comes,
can the hostess be far behind?

She loved order
but did not mind dust;
during her walk
grew confident the boy
was engaged in an immense action

by the English garden phlox and the delphiniums.
Man writes prose, poetry writes the child
prancing on his stick,
tutor to the man. She is trying
to make out his absence,

like the wasp against
the window pane
squandering its head
into light
at the close of their sermons.

The boy knows it is the last day for money
when he sees them kneeling before her,
without a doubt thinking they kneel unseen.
He comes upon them unobserved,
his heart is joy.

There used to be no house
hardly a room
in which someone had not died.
Here in the country it was animals
in the now-remodeled barn, remodeled yet still

that huddled red behind the homestead tottering
but fatherly. Think
of the medieval pictures in which
the death bed has turned
into a throne toward which

the people press through opened doors.
This is the way it is
in the hayloft now an office
sheetrocked, wide-board floors;
and that skylight

he loves to think of sleeping under,
leaves waxed with skinniness
in the rectangle of light and dust;
any item she wanted to get rid of
at the head of an aisle

or foot of the stairs; lettuce, chenille
rug, broken shade, that bunch
of plastic blossoms
bright with the courage of corruption—
stiff hibiscuses just losing color

from the leaks. His father says it is
not necessary to live, but it is
necessary to live happily.
Ah, the cold, the son is thinking, cold
cold as a well digger's knee.

GARDEN WALL

But what could they have meant, the old days, so small
they looked about to disappear? You heard
they were actually used, although from here
they come on like rooms of a doll house:
you'll love it, thinking what work it took to get
a daily sustenance. Quotidian broils

who are you, and masonry, what is your message?
A lummox in chambray, a lad in silk; bags in petticoats,
if they wore briefs no one could see to read them.
Still those five-star days are ours to hold—
though they're not good for anything and we
can't read the writing—essentially bric-a-brac.

What for example is this one saying
when we can make out only "full moon," and "time," then
on the other side, "autumn"? And isn't that "heart"
on the bottom? It all reads like a legend
running around the lip of the cup o' desire
overflowing with apprehensions, funky musings;

where do they seep to, down there on the floor?
Natural beauties make him sneeze,
he looks over the edge, gets really close, then
weeps a little, kneeling; tears at the edge of the bed.
O my, not halcyon days again,
credences singing everywhere, blooming

with the fields of dahlia and loosestrife! Then time
for the most important drill, time to go back
inside and think of the difficult and what it says,
inscriptions written in such a beautiful hand
and yet so difficult
almost impossible to make out.

FIELD AND STREAM

They want one of every kind and they
can't help it, it's an addiction,
the house full of novelty radios,
snow domes, stickpins, aquarium furniture,
Depression glass, Flow Blue. An example
of everything there is in the category
of your choice, mint copies of all the variant
bindings of *November Boughs*

or take Aunt Nell, her toothpick holders—
and then her last great passion, nut cups.
Just try to get a run of something,
they call you a completist. So
what if it is a desire to have—
if not *it all*—then all of one
shelf, or slice of it! But I
am not one of those who buy bears

chainsawed from logs by the roadside.
If I could have any Greuze in the world,
why bother to choose, for who these days
has even heard of Greuze! I'd rather
skim the cream off the top of the jug;
I am after high spots, I follow
the plough along the mountainside
and pause for a smile, or a mouse. I go

for field and stream and may have
terminal panolepsy; open
spaces afflict me like a passion.
I have done the physical things;
I take some bike rides so far out
in the country it might surprise you. I keep
stores of garlic, parsley, and ginseng
in the hollow trunk of yon ancient oak.

Even though a dark plank tilts
into the maw of earth just here
by the tar pits, and there is every danger
that my collection will slip into
that sink-hole, dire fosse, I fear
no evil but opening my mouth
and going on about origins
of the sacred; the bounty of nature.

Two

MAIDEN VOYAGE

Come down the watershed and at the confluence
gallivanting through a new landscape
where the days bark and you know it is over
find your place in the flood
or near it, and take care

not to catch rides; stay put
on the banks by the brimming waters
where there's a view, a folding chair; the cries of children
and rug dealers haggling at their flea market
safely out of reach on the other bank.

Days of suits by Athanase and Schiaparelli,
gone with ivory plectrums and bronze fibulae;
now cans and oil bottles, period action figures and
Binney & Smith crayon stubs marginally there but
long separated from the drawings they made.

Hopalong Cassidy judiciously tearing across dusty
hills of Southern California is what we are,
content so easily here in our globe
the flakes swirling about our grinny mugs.
We watch the dog cringe in the corner

when the boy comes home, and the moon
hide behind the withered town
with tear-stained windows, rumor
of travelers violent on the roads.
We need the mucilage, the desert core, go

weeping among unfortunate peoples,
Dante's afterimage like a flash on the retina
from another time, a pilgrim's progress;
making peace, or bidding to, from satchels
bursting with cola and leaf.

The truncheon appeared in someone's hand,
fell from the sky with a clank like a blessing,
heavy metal to the river bank where we waited
in the smell, elephant magnolia calyxes oozing
their odor as of rotten eggs.

PETERING

There are no exhibitionists anymore.
The radio stays on. Different buttons get
different songs but the off button's off
somewhere, out to lunch. Big people
own airwaves—well, perhaps he oughtn't
to put it that way since art must retain
a certain tonal rectitude. Say rather,
important interests are in play, while children
or other small fry come to hide the fax.

If you tell summer you just got back from Chicago
it will say, get to the right coast—or the left.
You may have a chance to be real. Chainsaw
is coming in to straighten this town out,
cut your idea of yourself down to size.
We thought we were famous enough being persons,
doing our work, composing T-shirts
for the kids. But when you lose
the job, a virus creeps. Nothing saves you

from the bland blank blokeishness loss
brings, the attendant dependencies, tickets
for lotteries, evangelical pep suppers,
choke chains reining ambition in, awareness
like a bit in the callused mouth. Soon care
will have everyone, unless your vehicle
needs major repair and isn't worth the fix.
Better be turned in on something new!
Full lots—thank God for that!—full lots

as many models as new moons, or stars
sailing across the western sky at evening
making their first appearances on schedule.
The new season brings a crop of faces,
younger looking, shampooed, tight

with the anorexia of victory, kick
boxing, the edgy pomades of favor,
ointments for kicking back, for bliss,
for getting born. . . .

DANGER, MEN COOKING

It's not ever but the one burner,
it's always at least four, the front burners
and the back burners simmering along too.
"Suddenly" something boils over but

it wasn't exactly sudden, was it, because
it had been simmering all along. Or another
starts out clear as maple sap and then
in a cloud of steam when you're in another

room watching *La Bohème* or taking a leak
"suddenly" it's combusted—and rock maple.
You find a crust going to rigid black
from chocolate-brown tar; have to chuck it

—the pan too. Such is life if we cook at all.
Better to send out for Chinese
and let them worry about it. You get these
little uppers too, cookie manna—like mine

the other night that said, "Heart is
pure, mind clear, soul devout."
Or yours, "Behind every lable man
are always other lable men."

FAUSTINA

Programmed for power, she got in her licks.
She told her side and pulled some haunting tricks
until she tripped, on sexual politics.
In the end, her wooden nickels would not fix
a single deal. Kicking against the pricks
at last buttered no parsnips at the Styx.

BRAIN DECADE

This is the decade of the brain you say
here at the end of the millennium striving
to get robotic cosmetics and surgery
out in the open where we can see them

for what they are. All the guys up in the cath lab
so nice suave too you know good
at small talk, imparting that blush of optimism
that makes the day go by like a nap;

one gets out, another glides away now an integral
part of dials mooning down on sheeted beef.
Now is the season of release and comfort
cots like Dodg'em cars moving through rooms

arranging fresh and more useful configurations
for those who stay behind and get along.
Do not be fooled by the nice weather, a voice
from the radio warns, do not be lulled into thinking . . . .

EPISTLE TO ANDREW

I know you're hungry again
but do you have to eat my couch?
It's taupe four in the morning, sun
already not far off, and you—
I got up and let you in! No,

strike that, I was up already
worrying about you; getting a glass
of water. Of course you're always
welcome for whatever and coffee
but don't have an episode on my couch

and don't pull the calendar off my wall.
I'll call Security. In my whole
breath I can't find a place for this,
it's not like anything beautiful, a cunning
garden or ancient gold, but it is

stunning, your hat, your tears, your hated
father, your hallucination about Rimbaud.
So, see you! You're off to New York
not Africa, and your heart is going to yell
a lot of shit from very high windows.

PARTY LINE

The Pope received Ito and his Japanese youths,
they gave him letters of credence; poems.
Gregory loved it but had no scroll written in gold.
It was 1585, he gave a consistory and had
nice Italian suits made for the boys. You never knew

though it might have made a difference
to find that out when you were fifteen. History
passes by like a migratory bird up there
at the corner of the sky, so far away you can't tell
what brand it is. Or an asteroid

half as large as the moon whooshes past the earth
ten miles per second, you never knew it happened
just as no one not even astrophysicists in their stretch
limos knew until
until they saw it coming hours before.

How can you plan the day that is so tricky
with things coming at you
out of a future, darkly random as it is,
or stepping away unnoticed into the past,
dark and uncertain as it is, slipping away

like the wedding guest who leaves
without going through the line and pockets
not only pieces of cake but silver to eat with?
Just imagine Gyatse the Dalai Lama
who steppeth not on sentient creature

but who drowned his regent in a tub of water.
Alack, we are all sentient beings, all
have to go up to the city to be taxed
for being who we are. The alarm
is ringing away but you still sleep. The possibles

arranged on the high sideboard of dream
vanish when a bird by the eave wakes you.
You hear song as the soles of your feet slap the floor,
know it for a cardinal's bright recitative, round
as a bell, in a tongue you know you could never follow.

A MEASURE OF THINGS

for D.L.

What you heard was the noise of the wind
at last making a difference in your stifled room,

a wind bringing the cry of crows and the distant boom
of thunder, like guns sounding among nations.

Threads of static crackled, more distant flashes
fizzing like soda. But still you caught their talk

through the wall in the next room, an argument
languid at first but soon observing market forces,

"you've made it pay to swear falsely by the ashes
of your mother, the silent constellations."

As her voice went on her frenzy lessened
when scarcely one ship came safe from the fire.

And he: "your world is big and awful, a gnawed bone."
Then the wind; and their room, silent as any stone.

SECOND EPISTLE TO ANDREW

And the dismay you beheld was not
what you beheld in others but
in what you had or had not yet
begun, friend there like a sphinx in your path;
not in the accomplishment
of one who went—and wrote—before
but in your mind, in your own spirit
hung, mirror in which you saw
an image of accomplishment
that might have been or was to be.
It was the shadow of your prowess
frightened you, and you grew deft,
making it out in the steady work
of another who, never dreaming
to overtake himself, kept working
half blindly, undefeated by
the ignorant program of his heart.

THIS JUST IN

The meal-trough before them and the whip behind,
stupid languor and the deeds of kings and scoundrels;
such antiquities, pop-ups of kitsch and book, ask history to
put on the boy's gorilla-snot sweatshirt & cut some slack for us.
How do you know the peculiar amalgams of evening,

sun through stained panes of the cupola's high lantern
ruby, cerise, emerald, pumpkin, gold, and then some
when the snowman leans like a gymnast toward the crust?
It's about time, she said. Waiting for the dog to die, well we're not
going to call the vet just because he does a biffy in the front room.

She changed events to a fantastic lie, everyone began
to forget the past it was like the flu everyone had it,
the forgetting how things went, a twenty-four-hour thing,
the past quickly over. I am convinced this dark is by Tiffany
look at the velvet shadows and the ruffled edges

pink like watermelon near the rind, frozen in a wave,
marble or bleached obsidian. No one will know
we are hiding here behind the portière looking remembering
the way it was when the curtains swagged back to glass stays
faceted to let a million fizzy rainbow glints cascade

over the silver and porcelain of the breakfast table
when the morning sun streamed through. But go to the mall
for a face lift, more rewarding on the slopes;
or punctilious. You think you know what you need,
that's the truth of the matter.

PURSUIT

The red camellia in a crystal vase
printed in platinum, another of Mapplethorpe's
exquisite floral compositions, a gist

that's not politically correct any longer;
little hints of lust that just graze
the eye; the idea of it, swelling, warps
my botanizing.
Speaking of yesterdays,
the head of petals shows
a yen for permanent tumescence, fist
shaken against the sky.

   The boy worked up into a leather—
   then shaved.
   Of every blooming flower comes
   a corpse.

Things that just happen irk
us then we try
to deconstruct our partner
tunnel through to the far side of shame,
disarmingly perishable as film unexposed.
What dangers lurk
in the backrooms of fun
and, fuck, it felt good to go berserk!
The choice demanded he decide to be
the raging artist or engaging jerk:
deep in the mineshaft of his will, he chose
perfection of the life *and* of the work.

DETENTION PERIOD

for C. C. Huang

This is the territory now, don't forget it,
you'll be down on your knee, if you do. Sign up
for work duty and a share of greens, or something
will give you away, possibly your own yawn.

Under present conditions—downsizing of mouths—
we must all report to each other on each other,
for safety's sake, mentors and comrades alike.
The moment in the car park appalled because

you overheard something about your life
and you had burned the box of letters without
reading them, as instructed. "He lived on Samos
one year, and one in London, following his star."

Those others, our instructors, have come to learn
with what might be called pleasure—if it hadn't
the odor of necessity about it—the full weight
of their bodies. Because today nothing has worked

nothing beyond the need to debase ourselves
before the edifice of our needs, it's only
when we have caught their attention at last
that we can get really friendly; win them over,

treat them cruelly with the cruelty we are.
You think you are getting by with silence or
cunning, then there you are, fingered—caught
by a judicious smile in the president's garden,

the malicious kiss on the boss's terrace
in front of the flowers just opening. You
fall there, wherever it happens, under the sun,
before the stationary blast of arrogance,

serious money being spent, never to be spent.
You thought the reason you worked so hard
to get through school was so you'd never
have to study again. O please, tell us again

how change is the main course in life, no
substitutions please.
     We liked the old place
with its little unremembered acts of combustion,

ideas rubbing on the stone of leisure, little
sparks from the flint of thought. But here they are
telling us yesterday is history, tomorrow
mystery. *Turn over,* they say; —*that-a-way!*

BLUE MAP

She was changing jobs but didn't have
a good reason. It was safe and paid well,
she wouldn't have to ship overseas—I'd
like to be able to stay in one place for a change—
the hours were good and it felt good

to help others. Yes, but—he said—being
an x-ray technician? You might turn
a cobalt-blue map of yourself, then what?
Something needed foregrounding; interrogation.
But he never knew what to privilege because

her life had always been so graceful, sylph-like,
demure; even that stint in the submarine corps,
diving with the crew of plaintive gobs
—a male world but a well-behaved one—
under the waves. What could he do

to convince her to be a country mouse
and live with him in Cincinnati?
The spirit of independence was
too strong in her, or she just didn't need
his quips, his spandex hobbles anymore.

WEDNESDAY

The most important thing was to control
—as Mao knew,
as the young in Tiananmen Square knew
and loved—the stone of authority was
expression of it. Mazarin, who despite thousands
of mazarinades sailed at him like cream pies at Bill,
knew he could stay in the deal—and did. Therefore
I blindfold you—
just a klutzy, quick *take*
on sensory deprivation during the drive
from Essex to Annisquam just so we both
can savor it (or if I had planned this,
vision-protective shades inked on the insides
so no one in traffic even
a fellow traveler would guess there was
anyone beside me but some victim of cataract fixation).
If I deprive you of sight on this little drive

—asking as always for your peaceful acquiescence—
you'll sit there both blind to the world and hanging
on my every swerve—as it should be—
you will give me this power in exchange for your content
and I'll take away the data, nasty trivia of everyday life.
Then (having asked you politely to remove them)
if I tie your shoelaces to your wrists and you
are helpless, beautifully,
—like a Chinese populace,
or Saddam's veiled muscle men
billowing onward before handwringing citizens—
I'll know what I am doing (and you're
doing shit) but
of necessity you can have no idea how I'll "go."

Just look at the sweet passivity
of armed soldiers in the square

48

absolved of decision making today
because of ignorance,
sweetness of unknowing in their eyes;
because of training, discipline, obedience,
the ripeness of belonging in their smiles.

*

Mary put down Mrs. Piozzi
and took up her sewing.
Fred made her squirm but she
had to be nice to him because she loved him so much
she had to do something with her hands though, and she said
our family is not accustomed to begging,
thinking how Fred was such a twerp and had
no pride, and was a nance sprig to boot. Well,
she had been laughing over the wonderful things Dr.
Johnson had said and now her day
was ruined, her savings, small as they were,
as good as gone and her mother's sock
spoken for now, to boot. These were the big
things they worried about. But they lived in a simple way
and did not have to worry about botulism
or the revolt of Islam.

*

It was up to others to topple the regime
unfriendly to their interests and so awkward
for their empire. It mattered not what papers
were being rustled in the next room—at first
it was the hum of voices in conspiratorial tones
whispering their little madrigal of greed, aggression,
righteousness. He didn't mind being blindfolded this way
and tied to the cold radiator—the weather
was really warm, the room stuffy, stale after those weeks—
it was the sanctity his captors presumed for themselves;
by their quick prissy steps and the clank

49

of tray down as if in a snit or hurry; he knew it,
the germanic periods of their languid discourse
about Classic Coke outside the door.
How much of a Victorian novel could he recall?
He hadn't had even a glimmer of arousal
since he'd been taken, let alone of prayer.

AIR POWER SUITE

Arching thoughts deny all but perfection
it is true yet the parabola of his smile made us
wonder; his carnations would astonish our banquet.
The feeling was we got down with it, went down;
but someone said—in the privacy of our den,
stale it was, but secure—how he
was a bastard, the bastard. The boss took off
his helmet to hear us, but he didn't because
he couldn't stop talking, and we were safe.
So too were the mobile doves floating around
the conference room above the white table half
the size of a hockey rink and twice as dangerous;

floated hovered and came to rest then on the
decorative ceramics fouling them a little
but not so anyone would notice, really, because
of the attractive way the glazes flowed and pooled
over the edges, like thoughts rising toward
the apogee of their expression, arcs that slowed
as they attained their last extremities until
they seemed as still as the perfection they implied.

WHAT CAN YOU SAY

Our case is not all that unusual, Lyle said,
with over two hundred parricides a year
involving incest. We just got so much
attention. Then he said they never claimed
they were chipping golf balls at the time, or the like;
then something about leading a life of service
and hope. At last I understood: how much
they loved each other and their mom and dad,
who let them down, O down, down low.
That man out there walking smartly along

arm in arm with a woman is fairly trim,
a little out of shape but muscular;
they walk past my window—they are not arm
in arm, after all—the sun comes out for a minute,
I see she is leading him by the hand. Behind,
two children trail them wearing black T-shirts
under little back packs, full of something heavy,
so that the kids lean forward somewhat as
they follow the man and the woman, who keep going
a little faster, wherever they are going.

BUT THEN

But then what if my desire for another life
came through, like a striped pennant or a sail—
blue, white, brick, orange—streamer spanking in sun
without a trace of air's hammerhead weights
pressing their dull spheres of pain down, down
on what will have been going to be a day
with nothing at all but loftiness and breeze?

Instead it's tacky, a certain cosmic sleaze
at work: he was about to sing a roundelay
but rumpled blue jeans on the floor made a frown
and he didn't think, with his regressive traits,
he could get into them—or it: he can't be one
unless he can be two—and look at him for sale
in the mirror; watch him dance; be his own wife.

THESE THINGS IN A GREEN TREE

1

Here hang the photos of children at hip height;
that they may see—not us; how thoughtful. Now go through,
bend down to these faces blooming
like a bank of flares far off—look at the doubtful
smile of one, like a boy with a sultan's
turban above his brow.

2

Doom, dark and deeper than any barn,
cracks soon, then gaming children, nameless, dream,
dream of a doorway, what it frames;
left home to jujubes
more or less, to solo cares. Just
loose fish now, sad dogs not aiming, or
trying not to, for the fires they will burn
in their quick flash, bangled, golden.

3

From kid death save them,
from felon blood, death
penalty boxes, the next camp, shaved skulls
out in a yard, sun warming pates slick and gray
as cut marble. Granular kids
mourn the gritty minutes of daylight—
for their buddy, nine days' wonder;
for the hidden, for what is done.

They smoke on the noon break and think
that a boy kept bald must be beautiful to someone.

IF WINTER COMES

A redhaired man in a rusty salt & pepper van

If you want to do something you have to do it yourself

Your mother said it was all right for you, he said

Your gift is your own responsibility

You can ride to school with me, he said

You have to do what you have to do

She described him as a Caucasian

An idle dalliance in Hades' playground

She said he had a New York or a Spanish accent

The essence of making is invention

She bolted toward a nearby elementary school

A stitch in time saves nine

Prior attempted abductions Troy area by a redhaired man

Most remanded, soonest mended

The man's hair was described as being cherry red

If higher powers won't help, the lower will

People phoned in license numbers on salt & pepper vans

You can swing it if you wing it

She said the van had no windows

NOT SO FAST

His life as pay-per-view entertainment,
tramping irreverently through the rushes and cuttings,
waiting for the climax apparently unable
to do anything about it, or that judgment day, a half-day
they were taught would come defining place,
and make them stand out from the grunts forever.

He hung out waiting for the good thing to happen,
a goddess getting copy in the weeklies
noting accomplishments, gifts to the community, more.
Overhead a jet ruffled the silence among clouds, distant,
as if pulling the blankets of sky more closely around it and going
distantly on, a fading snore; and that

was all. Even the wild geese seemed bewildered,
less sure which way warm was; ceased
honking at wrong doors in the flyway above his window;
forgot their flight plan together, settling the mill pond
like a failed joint venture come home to roost:
and left him to flies stammering in casements

looking for air, a berth, the light of leaves fallen; like children
leading their exuberant lives without the knowledge of
abandonment they would acquire like fading hair, a few
strands of gathered grasses in lilacs gone to seed, leafless,
empty nests, little chalices holding their waiting bowls
wide to the riddling light of cold.

LIVING HISTORY

Here it is then, the whole shooting match. Gratitude
for sunny days; the final week of the sale, that medicine.
I miss Felix, any old accountant won't do. Should I
choose to exit our domestic market, little heaps
of the earth's crust like silicon under those

many-striped awnings down on the square?
What bee will I get in my bonnet next?
I wanted to come from an era when
ivory was the medium for sculpture, not
a soap. Did it matter if a beautiful thing was

made by the ten thousand? Lots of something
lovely should have been nifty. Now—I waited
eight months for the plumber and he never
came. The faucet dripping, and he's been made
town manager. *There's* an apotheosis—and

a revelation, the raw-boned boots
I won in the race for attitude. Those boots were
National League boots! Now I listen when the man says,
"Everything is arranged in Palm Springs—true fact, sure,
and can be said about most any situation."

Whatever comes, comes down the pike at you,
ribbon of steel and tar and years shining
in the sun; miles like children, or the wages of "adulthood"
or the neighborhood that is eaten as the jolly
black town car hurtles down on you, bent on

arranging you as a short form. carefully filled in,
paid up. Lord a mercy! Those buds are opening
—at least poking out from their wands—peeking
into the sunlight of our century. As for me,
UV shades help, and the broad-brimmed

hat keeps me from mooning about bigmouth
dreamers in Melanesia, navigators of time with
yarns to spin among their scattered Solomons
and the wild blue yonder. Let me tell you,
they can tell blue from blue without half trying.

AND EVENING CAME

The way a diamond

              stud in the tongue

Of a girl I know

              thickened

Her speech.

MRS. WOOLF LISTENS
TO HER NEW PHONOGRAPH

People thought her eye was watering but
it was only the mote of clarity known.
There was an immediate joy in seeing
but it turned out a Camelot of sorts.
Taking her fences, she knew at last
follies of interpretation. Leslie, tinker and tout!
They all had to train, learn how to give
and take, but no one said what the training was for.

She knew a celestial spark when she saw one
and felt the brio of earthly powers.
Waking in a dingy room she found
an end of passivity, asking
how many selves she was—knowing
how faulty the bootstraps were, and would be.

TOUCHING BASE

At this end
it is hard to see
what it is saying. If
he longs for
a prime interlinear
the august crib
telling letting
it out, what
can he do?
An ancient gusto
comes across
him August wind
like a hand
on his neck or insects
red on scanting snow
and a certain
knowledge that
that crazing white
exsanguinating
crimson specks
is yearning—
a meta copu-
lation with the
world in which
it is all
sweetness, stretch
of one.

Day, baleful
and tender
soon all fleet
ferocious
enemy of bird
nimrod of
squirrel;

the attempt to
find something
of of—
the knee aches the neck
axial twinges at
skull wobble O
for a tent bag to rest
head against.

Man,
keep leeching
grime from
grain carven grain:
think

of that canvas
unframed girl
in ashes-of-rose
so lovely
lonely under blacklight
what a pity she
went so blotchy
leprous
with patching, that
pancake of restoration
where nothing
remained to save.

And a star
that star
soon quenchable
in the deep night
the starry night
of one, one waste
cindery end.

CHARACTER AS FATE

In Mexico we danced on the edge
where the saguaro cacti stood up
like billboards of cactus in the persian blue twilight of Tucson—
ah, the desert in bloom
lizards with spacegear helmets on our sill
and we in our deckchairs taking the winter sun!
Nothing to do but listen to wind in the cottonwoods and think
how this is certainly worth two hundred a day
yet that means we will have to leave
after, let's see, about three more days,
get up, throw our gear into the saddlebags
and fill up the old Cherokee.

Sea spray recalled the surf of snow
welling up as our sleigh sped onward,
washboard of packed powder giving the bells a shake
over the Dakota-like steppes toward the East
on whose scrub and buttes the tired sun
was shedding its light without conviction.
But we stood on the end of the pier
half a mile out into the murderous
glamor of the sea and looked back
with a touch of longing I admit at the waves
like pectorals flexing, crashing on the beach far away
and waited for the genuine helicopter, ours, to land
scooping us up into its gear,
the ritzy vibration and glamorous lift-off.

I nestled in my beaver and sheepskin
and went to the wall for my beliefs.
The state ran the camp for art
at first it was like basic training
to reverse the habit of compassion;
yet we resisted, life itself was
resistance, a kind of survival, a brotherhood.

The potato soup was cold as dock oil
but we were together every day
encouraging each other
under the photo of Scriabin doing the polka in a sun-dappled
    pavilion
with a ravishing girl whose head
turned away from the camera
and watched the whitecaps blink on the bay.

Few of us were left, though we supported
each other and went to each other's
afternoons. The nights
were silent as birches; moonlight tugged at our hair.
I was given a room with a chair
and the very bed that Solzhenitsyn had.
No one but us in the dacha, and a typewriter
on the deal table covered with lace
and the old fishwife crying *you havf your londge*
now glimb back to vork.

We often considered
the delights of travel, languorous terraces of Marrakech, picking up
important Straits porcelain for a song,
gardens sprayed with riotous colors,
the gold and diamond kerosang
that Hogan gave Shaidali.
We knew all these things, survived
all the regimes.
Exile no longer matters because
it is a state vestigial
as the appendix is to the body temporal.
Yet no one will believe
I am alive and glad here in Kuala Lumpur
where the State feels an obligation
to fund radio performances of work
by all living composers, while the books

burn quietly out back of the sports
arena, where cries go up like fireworks
and the teams smiling like bankers come
from America to compete.

IRON VERITY

Braiding the crop here with strands from the horse's tail
in the leisure he prized, his medley of groping and coasting,
he had survived. He passed the time
content to know there would be a reason to go to market
if only for the gossip, the old faces
the usual wondering sidelong glances, the
whispering how their leader had done it, how he
became the city and guarded the seven gates.
He saw how important non-negotiable play was:
he gave the commandant a smile then a smacker
caressing him too, a sort of Judas kiss on the mouth
when they gave him a membership card, gilt edged
security of sorts. Brave of him you say?

Brave heart, he was only one manipulating
where he could not prove; osculation
had been the preferred m.o.,
his dish of tea. The move had always been his
pawn to Q3, if you see
but that day he was just coping.
He did have to worry about the Brown Shirts,
he knew *that;*
in former weeks the concierge would not let them in.
Then there was no concierge.
They lived a life of comfort, discipline, recreational
brutality. But they had an excuse: the economy,

at required weekly rallies on the square
when group leaders cried how budgets
were at the gate. Yet re-education went on
staffed largely by survivors
who were made to carry papers, ever more
papers, until they dropped
or talked. Work progressed as a boar pisses,
in jerks, and some of them—lucky

guilty or productive, it came to the same thing—
kept on. When the cuts hit
there were entertainment rides; ceremonies
like an ongoing celebration
among the living. This is no tall story. Each of us
has something to sell, something to survive.

THREE

PIRANDELLO, PIRANDELLO

And Alice will not write "apocalypse"
or "divine" again. The essay's done. She's cutting
cut-outs now. Tonight, "Six Characters."
The solution was to choose, and now Tokyo

will claim her for the rainy nights and the hot wine.
Where phoenix-swirls exhaust makes roil outside
from pipe and smokestack, she will write a card
while she ponders the close of her poem on Prometheus.

She'll write one to the child. Soon she'll listen
to a temple bell. Recall the dated thunder
of home; the vacant hillside of Vermont.
But Alice is here, legs crossed on the Bokhara,

watching the child asleep, saying to herself
"Pirandello, Pirandello" over and over
as if it were the name of a bird; as if
it were a mantra, holding her single; sure.

CLEANING THE CLOCK

We remember our manner today
going from there, cool,
sweet, unthreatening,
the soles of our feet

daubed with sea tar,
wondering who was right—here in the sun
of a new day—what the departed had to say
to the present. No one was right

except the news;
the past hadn't a thing to say to them
the past had a heart condition
beta-blocker slowed to a snail's

pace, *pace* Aesop. Forget-me-not blue
drenches the globe like a paint ad
but if we look carefully
we find inky rorschachs of tar

on the shore, spume
of dollops viscous in the high noon of bravado—
caulk from some ancient trireme
out of the wine-dark sea out of the

canceled insoluble depths of what is sunk
faultlessly as the *Titanic*
out far in deep where tired claws
potter in darkness blind

to the slow currents or the shadow
passing over the sun
blotting the surface that flashes
and tosses thousands of feet above.

SYNAPSE

1

First notice cold, then heat.

Horns in the street bother him then
they're little; distant chord
he can't mind at all. Prick tunes in
starts up, leaves some e mail
then shuts down takes a break
while he contemplates weeding his garden

but nap instead.
Snaps snap, unsnap, little open jaws

or shut, congeries of buckles.
Finds himself a
dish for affables,
downtown crossing for systems.
Not gardens.

2

Lot of work to do scrying the way through
like a bit carving through 4 x 4
to hot-white core in which
selves most utterly,
selfly, reside.
                    Trees
blow the wind; it bends, peals under
forces. Train is hot

whereas he had thought to expect air

going somewhere.

3

You just then walk past a museum
look in at the blazers having dinner

or firemen at a fire in only jockeys
hoisting heavy rubber fatigues and boots on
while they finish quick bites

like young Trojans buckling on greaves
locker-room ball players not afraid
before the smoke

having beaten chance and theft
briefly giving true
lift to the day

nipples, rising
languidly
from brown aureoles of sleep
yearn in mind's eye as he

4

head for the E train avoiding
eye contact with dealer hanging in the men's

where he makes water then approaches
washing of hands—
jump when the automated faucet

makes water leap at him
hands when they pass near the bright

mouth, steel trim—& now to find
his didn't do anything and

feel himself not there—
is *not;* the hunch he

won't become acquainted with
some narrative acting him out.

NOT VISITING THE DALAI LAMA

In the dream, he longed to dream; a dream
that showed a placid river's mouth
with harbors on its auburn shores.
He listened to desire, lingering,
a lover on a porch of shadows.

He stood in the lower chamber, listening
close as he could to the room above.
Cupping his ear, he waited; heard
when Dalai Lama's laughter died,
his words. "Ignorant of bliss

the happy boy lays down his hoop,
takes up the spear; then dons the cowl
his elder wore. He bows—and keeps
the record of the tribe." How wide
grows thought, imaginary landscape,

the tomb of the stuccos of Cervetri,
hill town topped by castle walls;
where townsmen clustered, ringing temples;
houses with gear and trophies hung!
Reclining there on the high couch

the next-to-come lay slumbering.
Unmindfully did they descend
the staircase of their years. The throne
stood empty, yet it spoke. In his dream,
while a thousand seekers trekked, he stood

in the lower chamber. Would not go
into the vise of traffic. Knew
a mist; a rock; a niche below
the drip from rock sodden with rain.
Held one hand up, waving salute;

the other to his ear, attending,
knowing how what would come had come
in the light behind him pouring down
the steps into the torchlit tomb
where dancing, wine, and couches waited.

Secure in the dream, he stood at dawn
on the heaviest, gargantuan
threshold of smooth-dressed stone between
two viewpoints on his being: in
and out. Like sunrise Dalai Lama

was smiling over the hills at absence.
Hand to his ear, among the ten thousand,
he sought the rampart of a background
behind which rose the listening rocks;
more ships on the horizon; far.

BY COLD FIELD, BY WALL

These leaves that move in sunlight
from red to white to red and speak
of closure, need, and human
daring, frame the figure

a man in Massachusetts down
abandoned fields by drystone wall.
He takes a stand there, as if
to lose himself, his bearings; one

who lost the home port of desire
the muscle of his work
where now the drained leaves fall.
Save us from ruin sings

the painter. Keep him small,
a voice calls back, amid his brushstrokes
white and red and all but lost
among impastos of a day.

FOR JULIA, WITH A JAR OF LUPINES

Bring me a hank of roses, friend,
before the garden stiffens.

He had an alert sense of his own need
for material comforts and recognition.

In many ways none of this mattered
but the wine, the important feeling of texture.

Under the lavender foam of cirrus, swallows
looped; beyond trees, the pavement whined.

Against the heavy cream of enamel woodwork,
like a bat, the politics of abandon circled.

GROUNDS

Think about the positive
and negative space. Think about big
a little. Think about your relationship to the object.
Think of vast space, and intimate.
Think about the light being warm—or cool.
About shadows and the light which makes them

and if they are blue
or only pictured that way. Think about narration
and composition. Telling a story and how the scale
will come along with the tale.
Think about interpretation about
what Peter was going to say, what Paul said,

the history this is
and the language it is of;
about paint and slides, the lingo
of color, the lingo of paint, the lingo.
Think about thinking, listen up
to the ceiling, figured, grounded.

VALUE ADDED

No one knew what the stones like squatting frogs
signified. There they were, fuming in rows, out
of the ground; every critic had his explanation
or hers. But—we had to remember—they

came to nothing, every one; those large stones
out of the earth served the systems
of those who considered them, as explaining
something about the past it was important

for the explainer to explain. And yet
no one had any idea truly; there was no
basis in fact for any view of them, and
they remained like their origins—or like

smiling Olmec babies, sweet but ominous figures
come from the earth to reproach us, almost
cheerfully, for our ignorance—a mystery, just
as the probe of our feelings came up with nothing.

MYSTERIES OF UDOLPHO

Valancourt offered his hand
but Emily would not take it thence.
One hundred eighty thousand words
must needs come to pass hundreds
of sunsets before things work out for them.

And they no longer have to play
their cards close to their ah!
bosoms but show each other
their hands. All hands on deck, is it?
A full deck, you say?

It is not enough any longer
to reach out and touch someone;
ask Tom, cynical twin, just suspicious
enough to keep doubt upright
like a centerboard down in the drink.

Not enough any longer to keep one's hands
to oneself you may as well
go put your hand in his side.
This way to disease and starlight
forever on your sill.

Give me a hand he said and climbed
out of the hole. I respected him
for that openness, always. Unless
I miss my guess I saw the pocks
of nails where he had held them so hard.

THE DAY VAN GOGH VANISHED

Somewhere I left my Van Gogh *Letters*, three
volumes, heavy like a sack of groceries. Maybe
it was at the filming of Mitchum's life done in
costume—period brushstrokes, all
the scumble, scrawl, and pentimento
of a life; those colors, my!

Our last meeting was to be on the sadness of Theo
and life without theory that grew too innocent.
But first I stopped at The Russian Rock Shop and was tempted
by a big one that had already been reduced twice
and had a tag at one edge that read MAKE AN OFFER.
He had bone rabbits from Vladivostok too

and some old—but shiny—icons as well.
He said if I wanted an icon cheap I could
buy one of the new, but they had patina.
The smell of fresh baked noodle soup
wafted from Sammy's Noodle Shop and Grill next door,
I stopped in for some spicy bean paste noodles.

It was so noisy, everyone was talking;
they laughed over their delicious bowls,
a joyful place, smiles between mouthfuls.
So I decided to read but
found my bag empty except for a faux-brass swivel catch
from the hardware on the other side of the pizza

and Vincent gone. They would have complained
about too many letters anyway, and
that life-without-theory theory, but I
left a note about the books on Sammy's bulletin board, what
a busy place! I retraced my steps looking
for Vincent, the gold-and-black volumes, in every

cranny I might have stashed them
while stopping to take notes or admire
the fruit glistening on rainy Korean street corners.
The bookstore fellow was giving his lecture
yammering again but stopping to tell me
not to talk about my children but leave them

notes on the notice board; he hadn't seen my Van Gogh,
hadn't had one in years, let's see, three years.
Then he went back to his boring browsers: yes,
he said, it's time for me to make a mark
and publish. It began to surprise me, recollecting
where I was, and it dawned on me I had left my Vincent

under the table by my chair at home, heaped there
like a faithful but sleeping pet
because the books were too heavy and no one
wanted to be moved that way now, all that fret,
any more than I wanted to sweat
carrying him around.

AMONG BIKERS

He bestrode each gleaming chopper on the floor;
a kind old man, T-shirted, gave advice.
He wanted a bike his friends could not ignore
and learned how many cc's would suffice.
He found a beauty, and his heart grew sore.
The salesman said, if you must ask the price
you are not ready for a Harley yet;
for that, don't question going into debt.

Malcolm thought money but a spume that played
upon the heart's own paradigm of things.
Sacking his chauffeur, the great fortune made,
he took off tweed and linen, earned his wings
and dreamed how golden-thighed Knievel rode
into the burning air, imaginings
a bar made real when he, in leather clad,
could cruise the dark and feel himself a lad.

Both sons and fathers worship images
but those society approves aren't those
that animate a grownup's reveries,
but keep a leather or a chrome repose.
And yet they too break balls—O fetishes
that passion, lust, or simple prurience knows
and that all perks of status symbolize—
O little men who mock his macho enterprise!

Biking is celebration, tripping where
no one gets hurt when he knows how to ride
and satisfaction out of the rushing air
is beauty throbbing. No one ever died
a better death than with that power there
between his legs, warm cylinders of pride.
No one can ever tell you what it's like.
How can we know the biker from the bike?

DIVA

Her voice was like a bearded iris in full career
or possibly an Asian lily somewhat blown,
a tall one, but she sang *Delilah* well;
she could stand up to the Philistines or Placido like anything.
Her arpeggios were a breeze, her voice
was roomy and agile in the higher ranges
like a lady smoking as she gives orders to her staff lined up
in her mauve dining room, their mistress by the sideboard
where a silver garniture holds some of those bearded irises
freshly cut and with their leaves spearing in chevrons of *v*'s
like foliage in a Rousseau painting shooting up, reeds parting
to reveal a feline, playful but leonine—only
here it is bearded irises with a little stubble
from the calyx at the head of petals, little furls
of short hairs half congealed with scent
as if spore about to trail along the breeze—

and yet, and yet her voice was like a woman's when
in shade she turns from the Coke machine
in the office hallway at ten past 4 p.m. to address
her lover, one of the bosses, in careless whispers
whose high octaves can be heard all through the office
and echo even off the buildings opposite the windows,
the light of deep afternoon falling across them
and turning tacky, dun vernacular walk-ups
into glowing facades of possible Alhambras rich
in the salmon oranges of tea-time sunlight, the
gilt frosting of window panes gleaming gold above
the far-off muted horns of taxis below

that blend & even now harmonize with the liquid
soprano divagations of the diva's sweltering
hover over perfect, then possibly not quite perfect,
pitch, and in the climactic orgy of derision—put-down
party to rag poor Samson—Delilah's voice goes emerald now

among the general citrons and sulphurs of the chorus,
posse half into standing back, a backing off
as the lady of simulations, the lady of the hour,
sits down her loggia from her dogs
and slowly lifts the cloisonné container, cigarette box,
while turning her smile in the shadow of her hair
toward the adoring boy who only knows her
as Mrs. Warmee; knows her voice, the awning
that fans his day, the limelight, her high spike heels.

ESSENTIAL REWARD

Ibn Saud died thinking the world was flat,
though he flew to Boston once or twice
he knew what he knew, bought a rug, stood pat.
Yes, and hanging plants need to be watered all the time.

You have to water when you should be depositing
the paycheck. The human body can live four weeks
on its own weight in liquids, a cactus—
for twenty-nine years. What

a disappointment, and I don't have any
spines either, only a neck!
This morning is not going well but then
neither is my elegy in an age of plague.

Abdullah potted so well he could throw a wall
thin as broadcloth, but it doesn't comfort
the way it did years ago when we trusted
in the beauty of such accomplishment,

the knowing something could be done
that was almost too fine to be believed. I have to
remember the disk of how we preserve ourselves,
what now saves our particular image from obliteration,

flat and round and perfectly shining;
unremarkable, essential reward
and paltry in the stony desert of generations;
golden coin nailed to the mast of becoming.

BLUE PERENNIAL BORDER

for Geoffrey and Barbara

He could have sworn water was running somewhere
he heard the sound gurgling over the house
as if it were the shore and the tide
moved along through the tidal pools in or out
but nothing seemed to be on,
outside it was a sunny day, a perpendicular morning
with birds looking up the weather on their net.

He wanted to believe what she said
the crisp judicious style was such a convincing vessel
for her thoughts, those fresh
lucubrations enviable as timely rain.
But was she right about Parmenides and if
it was so in the past and the future as she said
did it also hold for the present? The present
might not count, but it was nonetheless there
like a dog in a town with a leash law, pet
that can't just be let go run but always
has to be taken on walks and then prevented
from barking at strangers it decides may be
invading his turf. You want to drive him out
to the shelter because he is taking up your life
but you feel affection, loyalty, a bond
with the animal—just so, you can't simply
drop off the present somewhere on Tuesday morning
and not concern yourself about it anymore,
you're too involved.

The day was good, the bath
someone was running was ready, or taken.
But his foot was numb
and it did not feel much like walking out on the pavement.
They had a new office—over on Lex—
but he preferred himself to keep the old digs
where he'd done his little deals

and where new clients could not bother him.
The old hotel dining room was just fine, though dingy,
though the construction outside made a racket
even at breakfast.
Out on the island he got enough sun
to get brown as a bean and in bermudas
could traipse with glad animal movements over the warm rocks.
Quietly waiting
for what the Marine Biology Lab had to say
he stood around poking the tidal pools with his rod,
listening to the gods; apparently they
sounded much like gulls.
He checked for tropical fish that coastal storms
might have blown from the Caribbean all the way
to his feet. Yes, he had heard about melanoma
but he could not let it stop him
there in the breeze where being was
and a swollen foot might not tyrannize the day.

INTRODUCED ORNAMENTALS

BOMBAZINE, WINTER WEIGHT

Keep the home fires burning with war
voices? Why ever not, she reckoned,
now that all was clear.
They pursued medieval mysteries still,
whistling in the grime, scouting
for turnips in the rain.

The deadly checking could go on
until the end of the new. Saddlesore
under the stars, their true selves—the sincere
or the prudish. Who'd make the journey
to a war that would never become silence? Only
the few, the good—on the brink of liberation.

TRUE SAND

Beautiful beyond repair—a fearful thing;
they strut and cast their spells.

Shedding a burden of childhood crimes
they strip and dive for stuff along the bottom.

In this game the holist is the villain.
Remember then, at the gate, you:

you are a different crowd, there at the start
of the scramble, ephemera's envy.

How happy once, to be in need,
for once content at night to cruise

the buggy forest of answers, at ease
to be hugged by strangers. Sorry, loves.

You cannot live like that anymore.
You gotta have sand. Sand always wins.

(for Lynn Freed)

YOUR NICKEL

It was her own fault, those edible shocks
one part of higher education:
a rag-picker's world, desirable dissent,
a touch of bohème: or hearth & history
housing the gentry in peace and quiet,
a saintly dignity riddling
and rambling on, predicaments nixed.

Slave to success? Well,
everybody wants you when you're bi,
slave to style or not.
Getting to be gray,
fooled or unfooled, a life or two
behind the aspidistra.
Or, falling off a ladder—

what could be simpler?
I'm so proud o' you
said the great equivocator;
it's all parade-ground practice.
One folk, honorary animals
in the undergrowth; one nation,
flowers for the furnace.

CROW

She had to get on the airplane
and run it herself.

The moon snail, lavender
predator, drilled into its meal.

She came in from talk
as a ploughman from the cold.

The crow was completely neutral
when it came to patience, and fame.

RULING PASSION

Meanwhile the raiders of the lost
logos found something cinematic,
something to feed the dreams, the disillusion;
—of power, pigs, the human body.
In the ranks of spooks
they were poets just like the rest:

dealing with something, um,
mammary and desire!—making
royal splendors out of
the ordure of things, of ruling
passions, wisecracks in adversity.
Then the colonial boy stood up and

with sheer ornamental persuasion
ran against utopias, summing up the spirit of the closet.
Of all the damnable chic, and this
trying moment even after he was shown to be
only a clown from the town!
Meanwhile the bards at the party

true poets of war
galloping over the past in modern dress
would have nothing of it.
A style of superiority was what they were
and a life in history
what they got.

RECEDING WHISTLE

Caught in the politics of denial
what he really meant was cold war in Africa
and chronic shortages
on the high seas of romance
where no man had gone before.
A ghostly check on the cult of charm set in.

A saint of the shirtless
he was against freeplay and carried on regardless
winning the last war
and convincing the ladies of the steppes.
A pieman par excellence,
he might have cost a king's ransom.

Within the waves' senescent day
he called back, "Nice work
if you can get it"—fine words
and false—then amid echoes
of a receding whistle,
"Darned if those who understand . . . "

NEXT WORLD ORDER

And all this strange weather
it must be the other coast
as seen from the chair of a bookish reader
somehow finding out about shortages,
beach lesion, star death.

COLLECTIBLE CARD

Starved for books,
the school without an underclass.
There was a polite probing of entrails.
The children of Ham

unlacing straitjackets
made heroes of our time.
Bomb, what bomb?
Coffee for everyone

looking for themselves
across the Irish Sea.
On the spur of the moment,
getting over the Plaza, they found

rooms of their own and secrets
in Tennessee. The priciest
funeral was a bargain.
It was as if they drank down blood!

Tap on shoulder: you shall have
no captain but me. Back
to the Holy Land, another Florence!
And mad about the French affairs.

MY NICKEL

No torpids' race, the party of evidence
was big already and swelled with flower sellers,
dealers, pickers & such. Soon
the myth of failure was definitely *in*
with Manhattan moderns, those
saints and scholars and cuddly vikings.

MARROW SPOON

Silver. Digit on an apple peel. A garden
in a rug. The idea that someone
would not eat his lunch. The fool,
as Homer would say. A simple affair

of carrying mulberry to the mill
and tie-dying paper to look like the spot
where chrysanthemums wept.
But copper. Looking over the sharp

edge of sour shade quiet as sheep radish
he came in with similes blazing. And fresh
garlic adorned his simple smock. He looked
innocent and virginal yes but then

didn't everyone on Colfax Avenue?
Light through the curtain-stays, gold
on the bindings, motes like samaras
falling through air on the polished field.

MARSE CHAN, TRACER OF LOST PERSONS

More difficult to push a stone, later
when he grew older and his beauty faded,
out from the pyramid with his bare hand
than to alter words or the position of them

like big pearls and little on a plate of jade
hearing them, seeing them on the white
field back to reality with a rough draft
of night snow and how serious the issue is

doing his rap about intellectual pooty
and other pondlike ruse, the drought

south of the Yangtze
snow in Sarajevo

for the Olympiad of blood and laundry.
He had to go into her account
and withdraw fruits and lettuce fresh
from the South; bells, dew on the garlic.

And still as his friend, who should know
and can get off how he wants on parole, would say,
out after so many years and considered harmless:
in Ch'u-chou people are eating people.

Now that he has a green card and youthful cut
he keeps staying to dinner, in spite of the roast.

TACIT BLUE

Code name of a secret U.S. Air Force plane that never flew

Like a shoe box with little wings
the toy slowly came down the runway.
If Beatrix Potter had painted a plane
for Mr. Nutkin, it might have been this.

The toy flies out of the hangar. You find it
on some grass, parked at a sort of tilt. You
pick it up, imagine getting in, pulling back
the stick, flying away like a bird. But why?

—Well you may ask. The good news is
models are fun, one joy you have;
a hobby. Fun. —Bad news:
the only thing between you and the icy cold

crevasse is Pastime 909, a model aeroplane
you build at home, the old Pastime 909.

THE NIPPLE AS A SEAMARK FOR HOMER

And *tout le reste est littérature*, he thought
noting with interest how the spear
continually homes on the startled tip of
the breast, he who is about to die
saluting the shaft with extended arms
as knees buckle, and the point passes

into the sunlight, nodding, red
and warm; how exquisite each wound is
like a rose pinned to the breast
in a half-Tennyson. Mostly
the battlefield is a court where men
win whatever it is they win

and go down. Take basketball
it's not a game it's life, the kid said,
the rest is details. He knew the Delorean,
his favorite, would last forever
seeing it was stainless. Yet one notes
how other ideas of favorite come

just as dear. The curio dealer said,
try this gold mirror box, expensive
but when slide this part back
here now see these picture, heh,
see here where stem of lotus
enter palace of jade, all

will be briss, buy this for your rife.
Things look so much fun at first
—a real toot—but when you get
up close they look as if
they are dying in some final,
exquisite, mortal shindy.

DOWN ON THE LEVEE

Out of the tunnel, raising my hand
for a trip with "children included," it is our turn.
Make it what you will, it is programmed
to be different for anyone.
I am you see with you here.
There may be a small dog and a child
but they are straying far from traffic
so we will go on without them
on our stroll to the Chinese market.

Above ground at last the sound of music a polka,
bouncy, canned as the seven dwarves.
We go up past the garage—joyance,
dancing in the streets! Do we have time
to join in? Thinking ahead to amethyst and meadow rue
there's only you and me now, hardly enough
to make it worthwhile; we must head to the river
where the wheelhouse helm-light glows.
But in the center of town an electric

billboard, flashing, says DESCRIBE YOURSELF
and we blush, faltering in our tracks
knowing we'll have to put in something
in order to play, go on, find out.
But we know it is all just for fun,
a train's cry from an old steam engine
announces the fact; our carefully planned
peregrination is after all a cruise,
these choices leisure activities.

Wear anything you want, you're on vacation!
We spend a lot of time naming things wrong
on purpose—an art of misidentification
working as well as anything and even
if we are definers at blindman's buff

pinning the tail to an abandoned donkey
or if I say something truly green to describe myself
it will include you too; there won't be trouble moving on
to the next stage, down on the levee in the morning

chopsticks floating in the wash like foam,
like an oil spill from the galleys of Asia.
But look there, across from the billboard,
that screen: the miracle of pictographs
from paleolithic caves—mute testimony—
inspiring by the sheer fact of their survival,
and what they could possibly have described:
animals fleeing, outlines
of human hands, outstretched fingers reaching.

NIGHT LANDING

The slow ones. Slow one. Touching the stone.

And the runner dreams of a world but never
        says it,
having fraternal contact with the road
             touching words nimbly
like the gravel he skims as he runs,
        touching its luminosity.
Goes a dance, hunting among clouds.

Others, whom words use, the difficult ones.
        The slow,
who find the morning,
                sudden chateau.

*

In the photo of Rilke with Valéry and the sculptor
Vallette, Rainer is smiling, a schoolboy stifling
laughter in class; or is it that he smiles
urbanely and wears a high collar, natty, chaste
in tailored tweed and new foulard cravat?

*

The continuum of past and present
blurs.
      "Getting inside."
                Consider bread
rising, rabbi says;
               Torah is like
a garment. Clothing that covers other truths.

*

The veiled presence emerged, like an insecure
and violent woman. Some say it. We must
remain in the dark like the swimmer swimming his lane
who does not know until it is completed.
He has no dialogue with joy to come.

*

                              Flash
of light gleamed all around
from his head as he moved, turned, speaking.
A light separate from the light around—
in the sacral darkening, in twilight,
the unbewildered dark. Turning
meniscus that enthralled me letting,
letting the candle I held
burn on, wax snuggle, melt down
my tranced fist.

*

It was the hairpin in his hair. Catching
light from a window in the rafters, pin
attaching yarmulke to his head. Sabbath
is separate from the daily work.
The light is separate from the light around.
A blue template of creation. Shall I
answer this demand with presence, as when
the tree topples unheard, and yet it falls?

The weeds grow onward with the wheat so that
they must be pulled before the wheat is ripe.

SECOND ADULTHOOD

He'd see a stringy-haired old man in town
pacing the streets. He looked just like
Alfred Tennyson old, every bit
as private, daft, self-absorbed.

The zinnias were chest-high that autumn.
The spidery towers of cleome
sent out their spiky beacons
taller than his head.

FALLING ASLEEP OVER
JAMES SCHUYLER

I was home early, had
this beef with someone awful
at the office. No one was home.
The dog had gone on a day trip;
a note said V had gone off
visiting her brother in Sharon.
I went out back, unfolded
my Taiwan lounge with the blue
tubing that sagged and lay back
in some maple shade and started
to catch up on James Schuyler,
which was encouraging: yes,
for a guy who writes about
loneliness so much
his poems are full of people.
Friends at least, if not
faithful lovers. Someone
is always calling, or being
remembered for having called.
Soon I was dropping off,

easy enough to do
on Wednesday at three, more likely
closer to four, perhaps
from being bushed, then maybe
just strategic withdrawal
from stress, the trivial little
wants of everyday life.
I felt drops, fat raindrops,
splat on my pants and
I lurched inside. By the time
I came to my senses, I heard
a downpour drumming outside.
Begorra, I'd left the book
out there. No doubt it was

soaked to its spine by now
but out I ran in the storm,
scooped Schuyler from the grass.
Inside I dried him off
with a towel and fanned the pages
by the fireplace although

I knew such proximity
to a source of sometime heat
was meaningless at this point
in a damp midsummer. I thought,
you knew how to deal with your
isolation and turn it
to solitude—with your
zen-like dedication to
those spotless details. How strong
and flawless the resignation
became; how sweet, I guess,
that hard fulfillment was.
Now when I open your book
the edges are rippled. That rain
had pinched and crimped the pages
like a pie crust; the little waves
were permanent—mild ruffles
firmly set—when I read them,
flaky now, crackling faintly,
dry like an excellent pie crust.

LAGNIAPPE

Forgetting it—the tsunami of the future

Clearing the way for its own perspective

Crashing against the coasts of memory.

DEEP POCKETS

The guy in hi-tops legs spreadeagled
facing the wall there stands—ah
he is pissing—and mad as the dickens about something he
turns on us passing near with attitude of

get the fuck out of my space
true Penn Station's none of our business
something that's nought to do with us
and anecdotal as hell is

yet goodness here too
confabs of zonked homeless
breakfasting by the escalator donuts a smile
the upstate hockey team exhausted

by their duffles and last night
still grab-assing grin and call each other
darling before they vanish down into a dark car
like Alice after eating the magic cake.

SMALL WONDER

And look, they do not quit living
with each other, one tall one short
and they are of different stocks
one has osteoarthritis the other
arrhythmia. Billy and Dee just keep

doing the tango. Look at them
out on the floor all smiles
outrageous moves. They partner well
and it is we who look on
envious, doubting, not

understanding. A sprinkle of plaster
in Dee's hair from the ceiling
of their apartment shines and Billy still has
that wall-eyed glance that makes him
look ecstatic when he grins as if

he is having a time such as you and I
only dream about—if that: because
we cannot imagine what it's like the fun
the spin to existence spending life
together gives. We're wrong, you know,

it's much more subtle now we're taught
to applaud. Let a thousand flowers bloom!
Be glad they have this news in hand as they
redo the loft with knotty pine, ice cream stools,
shutter-dogs from Kent (Connecticut, that is).

ROARING SPRING

The leaves are better than dominoes, they all come
at once. They deliver, fast. A minute ago everything
was burning and now it is shade. We are walking
down a gray road at night, thickets to the right
woody hedges on the left; before you know it
here it is, so unfair, in the darkness—

perfume and flowers and everywhere
what must be lime twigs and green leaves, little
upside-down hearts and clubs jostling together
on the breeze. Lord, it must be spring, an odor
as Loretta would say of young men just out
of the shower. Feel the terrible
bark of the forsythia, the rumble
of nights gone by and—you hear me—those to come.

DATE DUE